Stirrings of *Hope* & Other Poems

Haimnauth Ramkirath

Copyright © 2022 Haimnauth Ramkirath

All rights reserved. No part of this book may be reproduced or transmitted in any form or by any means, electronic or mechanical, including photocopying, recording or by any information storage and retrieval system without permission in writing from the publisher.

New Sunrise Press—Bayonne, NJ
Paperback ISBN: 978-1-7363733-2-3
eBook ISBN: 978-1-7363733-3-0
Library of Congress Control Number: 2022916548
Title: *Stirrings of Hope & Other Poems*
Author: Haimnauth Ramkirath
Digital distribution | 2022
Paperback | 2022

This is a work of fiction. The characters, names, incidents, places, and dialogue are products of the author's imagination, and are not to be construed as real.

Cover Illustration by Junior's Digital Designs

Published in the United States by New Book Authors Publishing.

Dedication

This book is dedicated to my siblings, Sookram Ramkirath, Mohan Kanhai, Mohan Ramkirath, Simon Ramkirath, Murlin Ramkirath, Shirley Dwarka, the late Henry Ramkirath, and the late Lakshmi Sankar.

"Hope" is the thing with feathers -
That perches in the soul -
And sings the tune without the words -
And never stops - at all -

–Emily Dickinson

Author's Note

This is my fifth book of poetry. This collection is intended for both young and older readers, and all who love the beauty and the mysteries of the natural world, and are fascinated by the greater beauty and mysteries of the human spirit.

Poetry can sometimes be lofty, complicated, and difficult to understand. There is an innate simplicity in style and language that shines through each poem in this collection. My aim is to make poetry accessible to the farmer, the bricklayer, the carpenter, the tailor, the nurse, the janitor, the factory worker, and all who want to enrich their lives with the music and rhythm of poetry. Therefore, the images and descriptions are natural and fluid, and drawn from the sounds and sights of the world around us.

In a world where the breaking news and images reveal the darker sides of human nature and experiences, this collection resonates with the perennial voice of hope that the light and resilience of the human spirit will ultimately prevail. But the focus is on the poetry itself—the music, the sound, the meaning of the words, the movement of the lines, and the use of imagery and poetic devices to bring pleasure to the readers, and sometimes to provoke, even shock, in order to create that spirit of mindfulness and awareness that we can live fully and totally.

These poems are written for the world. It's my sincere hope that people from diverse backgrounds, and cultures will enjoy this work.

Table of Contents

Unaccustomed Things 1
Oh, Little Stream 2
This Loneliness 3
The Call of the Beloved 4
Tracing the Stars Again 5
Hands on Blade 6
Spring Rain 7
The Roots 8
More than Human Eyes 9
Tender Red Hibiscus 10
I Remember 11
The Robin Returns 13
Lessons from the Lilies 14
A Veil 15
At the Edge 16
Dwelling on Things 17
A World Apart 18
A Precious Thing Lost 19
Partitions in the Mind 20
A Word of Cheer 21
Drifting Snow 22
The Bending Tree 23
An Outburst and a Clearing 24
Great Fish in the Net 25
Stirrings of Hope 26
Colors 27

Dared to Outrun the Sun	28
My Work has Just Begun	29
Details and Baffling Things	30
Unutterable Symphony	31
A Door Slammed	32
The Mirror	34
Flickering Candles	35
People of the World	36
Ten Thousand Eyes	37
The Squirrel	38
The Private World	39
Bubbles	40
On the Wings of the Wind	41
Walking Alone	42
The Measure of a Delight	43
A Parting Gift	44
Insane Readiness	45
The Fallen Oak Tree	46
Untouched by Time	47
Unlearning	48
Just for a Day	49
Holding a Pebble or Two	51
Telling Stories	52
The Blazing Chariot	53
A Stillness	54
Don't Give up on the World	55
Winged Beings	56
Butterfly on Shoulder	57
Clogged Drain	58
On the Porch	59
On Charts and Horoscopes	60
That Wild Joy	61

A Little Blue Speck	62
Gifts to Unwrap	63
A Strange Brightness	64
While the Falcon Soars	65
This is your Day	66
Such Sleep	68
Piling Up	69
Little Things	70
An Accord	71
The Giant Redwood Treese	72
Near, yet Apart	73
The Call of the Trail	74
Faces	75
More than Rest	76
Mist-Laden Songs	77
Light Steps	78
Little Butterfly	79
A Rare Picture	80
The Atrophied Heart	81
A Little Earthen Lamp	82
They Work and Build too	83
What's in a Walk	84
A Smooth Slab of Rock	85
When the Pink Lillies Die	86
The Dawn	87
A Stirring Speech	88
Unseen they Roam	89
Battle Cry	90
Lost to Time and Season	91
How the Trees Pray	92
A Sweet Forgetfulness	93
Along the Pavement	94

Moment to Moment	95
A Defiance and a Flair	96
Voices	97
Measure of a Day	98
He Planted a Tree	99
Hands that Nurture	100
The Swallow and the Seasons	101
Bare Fists and Feet	102
A Dream	103
Portrait of the Soul	104
The Search	105
Scattered Things	106
Some Unfinished Work	107
Medals, Insignias, and Ribbons	108
The Train Arrives	109
Such Scenes	110
Molten Love	111
Flayed Tree	112
Lines on the Forehead	113
A Lost Song	114
More than Words	115
Things Seen and Unseen	116
Monuments of Love	117
Not by Words	118
No Story to Tell	120
Love's Pain	121
Over-Wired	122
Listen	123
Along the Shoreline	124
New Year	125
Autumn	126
This Strange Altar	127

The Band Plays on	128
An Affirmation	130
My Love	131
New Eyes	132
Entrenched Feet	133
Awaken by Songs	134
Unfeeling	135
Cell of Rage	136
Fire and Blood	138
To Kiss the Deep Waters	140
In a Saffron Robe	141
The News!	142
A Cap and a Gown	144
A Strange Poem	145
Phantom Forms	146
A Little Knowing	147
What's that Love	148
The Old Man and the River	149
Can we?	150
Heat Wave	151
Out of Tune	152
When you Walked in their World	153
A Rush and a Splash	154
Beginnings	155
To Write and Erase	156
Songs of Hope	157
Unbridled Waves	158
A Line Above the Waters	159
A Ship out There	160
About the Author	162

Unaccustomed Things

Frantic calls of doom in every land and clime
echoed through the corridors of time,
and though we cut them down like weeds
still blight the hallowed ground and mock our creed.

The good Earth has her ways.
Ill-fated patterns etched on nights and days.
Eyes in the storms frenzied and wild—
the gathered woes —the elements we've riled.

There's little of that fair wind.
The tides on storefronts; the forests on fire.
On every hand a singe,
and unaccustomed things feed the hour.

There's something amiss when a mother shows an angry face.
A love that can no longer wait
but needs to raise her hands—
her fingers pointed at our faces, our vexing ways.

But the Earth is frolicsome and young.
She alone can stare all day at the fire in the sun.
Stars in their passage gaze at her lovely face:
she is anointed with heavenly grace.

Oh, Little Stream

Oh, little stream with a gentle lively rhythm.
A mean rock mocks your rousing movement.
It looks you in the face and blocks your way.
Don't just lament; don't just stay.
Don't wait for someone to build you a stairway.

You have the birds and the woods to greet,
and the plain's parched lips to soothe.
Step aside the stingy rock and move along.
The world will reckon you wise and strong.

You need to know it's not all groovy and smooth.
There's work to do—undergrowth to bend your way through.
Don't just stand and stare at wine-filled grapes on the vine.
You need to learn the world's a little less kind;
look to none to fend for you whether the day dreary or fine.

This Loneliness

The flowers on the windowsill have faded.
Dust have gathered in the living room.
Cobwebs dangle at the corners of the ceiling.
The drums, cymbals and guitar are silent.
What has exacted this wretched obedience?
It's the loneliness that haunts your soul
and makes your world a bolted door.

It hides the face of the resplendent sun,
and those fancy colors of which you were so fond.
When a faint courage enters your being
and you venture to hear the love birds sing—
it follows you along the dusty trails,
and the city's thoroughfares where the music blares.

It cares little whether you're with the crowd in the mall.
It's in your heart; with every fearful beat it grows tall.
It suffocates your dainty ways;
rips apart the hours of your nights and days.
It's a gruesome thing that would feign a smile
to see you crawl another mile.

But in your loneliness— you are not alone—
if you could only know
ten thousand hands reaching to you:
a thousand suns blazing for you.

The Call of the Beloved

We swim across wide, muddied shark-infested waters
to meet the beloved at the silent midnight hour.
See how the mountain bends its head
to give swift passage when we heed the beloved's call.

When we pour our love on a bed of flowers
it's not like the measured flow of oil,
but like the mighty ocean that drenches body and soul
with laughter; forgetfulness of the hour.

There must be some void in a love shorn life.
The song bird is alive; love in the heart abides.
In the sweet embrace of the beloved we're reborn;
we're awakened to another time and space.

The currents of the Cosmos race in our veins.
Let us celebrate with drums and cymbals—Nirvana on earth.
And though Death may mock this short-lived bliss:
on our cold white bones the imprint of a warm kiss.

Tracing the Stars Again

Seen enough of the world.
Would rather be like a child unacquainted
with the dogmas, rituals and beliefs of humans—
their stories breeding fears of dragons and demons—
standing like unending columns of mist that would not lift,
barring the sky, the sun's eye, a falcon gliding over the cliffs.

When I would rather trace the stars with fat crayons,
feel the soft dew-laden grass, the first flowers of Spring,
greet the gushing streams and scan the fork in every limb—
what charm and what freshness to the heart
in these discourses, these conflicting arguments
like loads of timbers on the mind?

What's the solace in this haste,
these steps that bruise the face of the pavements,
these unending glum pages to scroll and stare
and these narratives of human unfeelingness that exclude
when the child longs for every flower of another color and kind?
What can this meanness in spirit and stride gives to the effusive heart
that longs for the seagulls' call,
the fishermen's joy bringing in the haul?

Hands on Blade

This life that beckons from all sides—
the only life we know.
Should we not take it in full measure
even when cruel North winds blow?

Many withdraw from the passing scenes,
shut the windows and bring down the screens.
Is it not better to be in the wild wind with hands on blade
than safe from life's travails in the shelter of a cave?

It's not for the faint-hearted to see waves batter the shore,
and chandeliers swinging when a faint tremor rattles ceiling and floor.
Watch horns interlocked, the struggle and the gore
and taste from the cup of gall that overflows.

When the raging tempest is all that life can show;
when ill-fated birds smash the windows—
braver the blood-stained face than the slumber of forgetfulness:
the refusal to look at life straight in the face.

Spring Rain

Come, sweet Spring Rain.
Beat down on roof and windowpane
that we know you're around,
and riding on the shoulders of the wind
to spread cherry blossoms on the sacred ground.

Come, sweet Spring Rain.
Wake up every stream, pond and lake.
They need to look at your gleeful face,
and rejoice in your bounty that makes them to overflow
with the jollity that's in every drop you throw.

Come, sweet Spring Rain.
Your steady amorous beat at night
makes humans and beasts to think of love's delights.
And when you pour all that's in your heart
behold a clearing as flowers glisten in the sun.

Come, sweet Spring Rain.
You bring the magic spell
for hyacinths, tulips and daffodils to bloom so swell.
And wherever you go you leave a linen-laden freshness
that lingers long in the human breast.

The Roots

They crawl around jagged rocks in the silence of earth.
They seek the vigor of depths that spills upwards.
Takes more than a resolute will for the roots to lay a network
that forces its way underneath sleek highways,
and for the clouds to wonder what power holds the tree
so high to look over cliffs and gaze at the mighty river
like a lighthouse that watches over dark deep waters.

The tree at that dizzy height
stretches far and wide to show its might,
but the roots crawl deeper to keep a stronghold
lest the stalwart tree in its pride dares to mock the raging tide.

The tree never seeks to deny its roots or give them cause to cry.
It knows that in youth and in age they open wide the gates of life.
And in the ill winds of a storm the roots are strong and steady,
like a fortress overlooking the city, like anchors in the deep blue sea.

More than Human Eyes

On a celestial wheel whirling beyond the edge of space and time.
But you would need more than human eyes.
Still, you would be bewildered and dazed
to see all at once ten thousand suns ablaze.
The beginningless dance of a million hues of light,
and in one place to stand: shining myriad forms,
unending galaxies yet to born.

When you would see yourself, all beings and all worlds
hurtling into the gaping mouths of omnipotent Time—
you would beg for the divine vision to be taken
for you to see the little house beside the lake.
To behold the beloved standing at the gate,
the familiar faces along the street
and children dancing after the drenching by the sea.

Tender Red Hibiscus

The innocent, tender, red hibiscus flower.
What ill, what wrong, what evil has it done?
A thing of beauty that smiles at the deep blue
to shrivel and cry in the burning sun.

What grudge against a gentle flower?
It brightens our days; colors our frenzied world.
See how it pines for the rain and the mild wind.
Who would not sigh seeing this undeserved pain?

It cannot run from the overhead sun and hide in a shed;
it cannot wait for the slanting of its rays.
When the old man looks at its bruised face and cries—
he decries the Universe for the disdain.

But I hear the drums of thunder; rains are pouring.
Tomorrow the hibiscus will be smiling.
Tomorrow the hibiscus will be smiling.

I Remember

When my thoughts drift far away in the wearied hours of the day
they go back to my childhood—
I remember it as if it were today.

Every puddle, every pond, every pigeon called me out to play,
and I knew every patch of the soft dew-laden grass.
I remember the painter next door,
and further along the carpenter and the farmer,
and everyone I knew—a friend or an elder to lean on.

I didn't run from the sun; it probed the pores of my skin.
It hardened layers of mud on my feet,
and (with a stern look) healed bruises on my knees.
I wished it had watched our fun,
and stayed a little longer to prolong the day.
In the rush of sweet play I bemoaned fading days; I hated shades of gray.
But when the rains came in torrential downpours,
I sent my little ships to trade in spices in strange exotic shores.

The song of the kiskadee sent a thrill in my heart.
Tadpoles in the pond were a string of black pearls.
I raised my fists against creeping shadows on the wall,
and stormy winds that made the paintings to fall.
But it never came to me that the human heart could contain
such wretchedness as to gouge the eyes of the mockingbird,
and besmirch the wings of the majestic monarch butterfly.

And more than books, my mind grew in that greater classroom
where the scent of wildflowers mingled with the aroma of fresh earth,
and every sweet dream preceded by the pounding surf.

The Robin Returns

Leaving the warmth of a cozy barn
the robin returns to sit on the hapless tree.
It is ready to sing another song,
but who will listen when the chrysanthemums are gone.

The robin does not mind a blast of November's chill
to show its fidelity to the beleaguered tree.
It remembers when it was a fledgling longing to be free.
The tree watched it grew; it yearned to kiss the vast blue.

At the urging of the tree it broke the wind.
It looked down on miles of plains and raging sea,
and when it rained, came back for the shelter of the tree
to dart from limb to limb and many a tale to sing.

But from its heart a burst of rage
at the hands that stripped the tree of its foliage.
What insolence! What manner of harm!
The tree bereft of cover to blunt the edge of sharp icy blades?

And what a spite to grab and twist its limbs.
At night the tree a ghost in the howling winds.
Who mounts a protest; who sends a blanket of care?
It's the robin that knows the undeserved pain the tree needs bear.

Lessons from the Lillies

Behold the beauty of the water lilies
and how well they live in unearthly ease.
They don't dwell on the mist that's gone
or worry about dark clouds over the pond.

Though they rise from muddy depths
their petals show no trace of slimy regrets.
And when at night they rest—
no thoughts of tomorrow crawl on their watery bed.

A Veil

We never really see the graceful cedar tree,
a wildflower, gull over the silent sea,
a clod of fresh earth, dew on tip of a leaf
and the petals of the lily that open by degrees.

The eyes brighten at the rapture of the rising sun,
but bedimmed at the ubiquitous columns of steel blocking the clouds.
They feel the pain of the drab news in town,
but rejoice at the crimson sun going down.

In our hurried ways we have little time
to look at the wonder of things around.
And when we do, it's a passing glance at the scenes
and not a purview into the heart of things.

A veil lies between what we see
and what're revealed to the bright eyes of a child that roam free.
The selfsame veil that hides the resplendent sun:
we walk in storms when there should be a jubilee.

At the Edge

The tiny bird perches at the edge of the roof.
It looks up at dark rain-bearing clouds.
It looks down at barbed wire fences and nets to ensnare.
Still, it sings a sweet song as if unaware.

And what threat to a thing
that lifts with breathtaking ease on angelic wings,
whose little heart breaks raging winds,
crosses stormy seas and soars over mountains.

And we with bigger hearts—
not a stirring in our breasts
that like that tiny bird we too can lift
when at the edge of life's precipice.

But we walk with fearful steps
tethered to a thousand timbers
lest we look too far beyond the rocks' edge.
And we would decry as demented
those who implore us to think of flight:
happy in our domestic walls to live and die.

Dwelling on Things

The river, revered and feared, flows unfettered and free.
When in turbulence she batters the shore
it's at Nature's behest,
and not from any vexation or spite boiling in her depths.

She remembers her pristine years; she grieves at our wanton ways.
But the river does not dwell on our meanness
that suffocates and makes her pant for breath,
and blights her face with plastics, aluminum cans and toxic wastes

A little dwelling on vexing things—lifted with the mist.
A brooding when the day is fine; it's a wretched adhesion to the mind.
It's the dwelling and dwelling on things that haunts our days,
and lays spikes of the cactus on our pillows at nights.

But we roam unbounded like the bright eyes of a child;
we venture to shores no river knows
and what unbidden joy flows:
when no wretched groove dug deep in the mind.

A World Apart

A hundred miles along the trail;
no elegant suit and pompous air.
No rich carpet or a ten-foot cake;
no rush for the train, no traffic lights to stare.

No deceit there; the river is awake.
The pebbles show their faces in the lake.
No layers of paint on rotten walls;
the wind knows the leaves to rake.

No sweet talk there—then the fall.
Along the trail the pilgrim's soul calls.
No glitz of metropolis; no frenzied hearts—
a giant red oak on earth sprawls.

No jackhammers there where warblers dart,
and gulls glide over rugged cliffs.
A hundred miles—the trail's a world apart.
A place for the wearied soul to rest at last,

A Precious Thing Lost

There're things I have lost along the way.
The most precious—the joy of children at play.
When I look at those sweet untroubled faces
I dread to think of the measure of my loss.

What have I garnered from these seventy seasons
compared to their ebullience and their innocence?
What has that winged-chariot robbed me that I long
for one day of their uninhibited frolic and play?

I am wearied of vexed faces, raised voices,
greetings and embraces where hearts never meet,
templates to ensnare, these grim stern walls
and dark shadows lurking in every footfall.

Roll back the years for just one string in my heart
to quiver with the sweetness of children at play,
and when I laugh—it's no feigned laughter,
but one that gushes from the heart of a child.

Partitions in the Mind

When darkness was born it gouged its own eyes
that it may never see the faintest trace of light.
And when it fills the sacred space
without a lamp our eyes are dazed;
we feel and grope our ways.
The breathing of the raven sends terror to the heart;
we brandish our swords at sleeping grass.

But when darkness lodges in the human mind
no lamp—not even the sun—can suffer it to decline,
to walk away or run before the ill is done.
It fetches the burden of nescience; it builds partitions in the mind.
Would besmirch a flower of another color and kind,
muzzle the drums of a distant land
and close the ears to an unfamiliar beat and rhyme.

A Word of Cheer

A word of cheer to a stranger, friend or passerby—
count it as a thing of value
though not as enduring as a planted tree,
or a well dug in a far-flung country.

We may never know the measure of its worth;
it's bound for the credit side in the ledger book of life.
And if the word is never said,
but you send to another a thought of goodness:
that sweet impulse brings a brightness on your face
like when you raise your hand to erase a wrong.

How little we know of the battle raging in another's mind
more vexing by the icy winds of our unfeelingness.
But a word of cheer—a balm that heals
wounds not revealed in harrowing incisions on skin,
but wounds deep within the psyche of a human being.

Drifting Snow

The game the furious wind plays with the snow.
Cause them to drift and dance in this passing show.
On the porch and steps not one flake—
just below ten feet of snow.

Who for sure knows where the wind will toss the snow;
where it will leave not a trace to show?
There's much glee in the wind; it moves with a child's whim,
and in a sudden blast takes from one yard and dumps in another.

And we listen to the wind to hear
if the snow will come in heaps along our way.
But it has an uncanny device to defy what we expect:
the wind rides at its own behest.

The Bending Tree

To the time-honored river the tree bends.
A lonesome message every leaf, every limb sends.
You lovers meet, embrace and mend your ways.
The staunch tree never leaves its appointed place.

A greater resolve the river never seen.
To wander what's this unearthly thing
by force of will to bend its limbs
for love so true yet so unerringly grim.

An Outburst and a Clearing

When the sky opens in a sudden torrential downpour
with explosive thunder and forked-strands of lightning—
there's no time to show a homely face,
to think of the fate of tender trees and shrubs,
seeds sprinkled on swollen garden beds,
ramshackled huts along the river's bank,
the concrete on the sidewalk just poured—
it's a venting and a rough handling of things
sending infants to their mothers' bosoms.

Nature loves a quick outpouring
and a clearing—perchance for us to see the sun
as if the dark clouds were never around.

Why then keep holding to that boiling, boiling within?
Let go—as Nature does
when every rain drop beats hard on ground, roof and windowpane,
and an inundation breaches every dam.

It's time to unlock that seething current.
It's not good to keep things festering within.

Great Fish in the Net

The braided nylon twine—a bundle of mesh,
but sweetly compliant in the fisherman's hands.
On earth, a wearied look, a tangled mess;
in air, the open net shows an elegant face.
A lovely pattern as it kisses the lake,
and sinks as if it were a wreath of lead.

It settles deep in the lake— the fisherman awaits.
The cord tells of a fierce tussle;
it tells of a great fish in the net.
No script to follow; no time to rattle the brain.
The flags of battle unfurl; no time to drain the last wine.
In the blazing field of action—a wily warrior born.

The battle loud and long, cruel and bloody;
fish and man like buffaloes locked in horns.
The slippery fish defies net, hook and lashes to body.
It seems for this the fish was born strong
like a falcon that rips the cage of captivity,
and springs into open air with unbridled majesty.

Stirrings of Hope

Where have the gaiety and laughter gone?
It's the season of carnivals,
but I hear no songs, no festive beats of drums
and no spirited footsteps along the city's streets.
I see no tents of revelry; I see no colorful flags and festoons

Look at the freshness of rose petals on the river's face.
Restless streams in the woods tell of no weariness.
All nature ablaze with colors; the air tender and gay.
Why this unease as if tempest-tossed and in a daze?
Why this dreariness of spirit when the sun stretches our days,
and frolicsome winds call us out to play?

The buttercups cease not to bloom when dark clouds loom,
nor trees run for cover when cruel winds tear off their limbs.
In the song that's life there are notes of sadness.
The drums beating slow; the music haunting and low.
But the drums will race with strings of the sitar
to tell of a joy that's unshakable in the raging winds.

A joy that has no kinship to our parochial ways,
but abides in the heart from which it springs,
and gives a brightness to all things.
It has a liking for those stirrings of hope that make the cardinal to sing
long before the gentle reeds sway in the morning wind.

Colors

Splash your garden
with the splendor of many-colored flowers.
See the steady stream of admirers
as bees, butterflies and birds gather for a festival

Look how the flowers converse and pray.
A glint in their eyes when they lean on each other
in sun and passing showers.
No forbidden walls of unfeelingness in their breasts.
They breach the limits imposed by humans—
they ride on the wings of the wind with their fragrance.

Behold how they embrace and kiss
when a mild wind breaks the stillness.
And when they burst in a profusion of colors
the weary world looks but then rallies to kindred voices.

There's hope the day will come fast
when we will fill our hearts with colors
as the garden swells with flowers,
as children play with colored chalk sticks on the sidewalk—
a blending and mixing the world never seen.

And then perchance we may cease to think, see and talk of colors,
save that which shows the LOVE and ONENESS in the human heart

Dared to Outrun the Sun

If you ran after a butterfly when you were a child,
and sent your little ships to brave the seven seas.
If you danced when drenched by the rains,
and the scent of the sweet earth ran in your veins.

If your feet were muddied to the knees,
and you looked at the river from the top of a tree.
If you followed a stream in the deep woods,
and sang in the wind with buttercups and reeds.

If you tumbled down from a hilltop,
and poked your fingers into the holes of giant blue crabs.
If you listened to the melodies of the Kiskadee and the Blue Saki,
and waited for the gentle manatee to surface on the rough sea.

If you did these things—
you had more than a sweet childhood;
you had more than a little fun:
you had dared to outrun the sun.

My Work has Just Begun

It ravaged the shoreline, wrecked homes and uprooted trees.
The overpowering wind thought its work was done.
Then was awakened by ghastly voices,
and summoned to more work in a far-flung town.

It climbed fences, and ran a mile along ghostly ledges and gates.
The lonesome vine thought its work was done.
Then was startled for a while
when told by the eerie wind to run another mile.

It flew over forests, vast stretches of mud and sand.
The tiny warbler thought its work was done.
Then the frigid air whispered to it with glee:
it needs to cross the sea to see the warm sun.

And wells I dug; I gave the harvest to the poor.
I too thought my work was done.
Then a hungry child knocked at my door—
my work has just begun.

Details and Baffling Things

Nature gives to things details intriguing:
stripes on zebra's skin, veins in a leaf,
colors for chameleon to deceive,
a thousand glints on faces of a diamond,
patterns on every shell tucked in the sand
waiting for the sweet touch of a child's hand.

What are the best of our designs
to wildflowers on fences interlocking with vines?
What are the best of what we make
to the honeycomb, robin's nest, spider's web?
And who with needle and finest of glittering threads
can fashion a fabric like the wings of the monarch butterfly?

And what artist can match Nature's symmetry and flourishes
from immortal tireless hands with deft light touches
that give the world the beauty of the pink lotus,
rich light veins and endless textures in marble and granite,
and undulating sands when the waves have gone?

Nature gives to things details intriguing.
Places eyes of fire in the minutest things
like a virus with a thousand fearsome faces to mock our wits,
and makes us to think if it's ever worthwhile to defile
or look with baneful eyes at Nature's baffling things.

Unutterable Symphony

PAIN and ILLUSION
and unending, unbroken AWARENESS and BLISS—
like infernal regions, like paradisiac realms of eternal springs,
like the darkest of nights, like the brightest of days—
far apart and unrelated like they could never meet.

Yet, not so far apart and unrelated—
to stand side by side on the middle of a vast battlefield
where two formidable armies were arrayed.

And there—
Time compressed to the span of a sacred dialogue.
And with one Breath of the Universal Spirit:
War and Peace, Birth and Death,
Joy and Sorrow, Light and Darkness,
and all the dualities that permeate the human experience
reconciled and transcended
in an unutterable symphony of infinite harmony,
and a crescendo of such awesome power and glory
the human mind and heart could not contain.

And when it was over
the human spirit rid of its primordial weakness:
awakened to ever expanding circles of bliss.

A Door Slammed

Malignancies in the body, maladies in the mind,
but where were they before their insidious intrusion?
Little we knew they were heading our way.
Little we knew we made room for them to stay.
Now they would not just walk away.
Each day they grow and sap our strength.
We wage wars against enemies entrenched.

We swim against every raging tide,
climb every mountain and cliff,
face the nakedness of every heinous assault,
walk endless miles along the routes of wearied caravans
and fight for another hour—another glance at the mighty river.

But what battle can compare to this:
when the mind is laid siege before a voice, a fist, a blade is raised.
When the door of memory narrows each day
until it seems as if slammed on one's face,
and the harrowing prospect—it may never be opened again.

When every minute gone like it never begun,
and loved ones like faces never seen.
When the mind has lost itself and the throbbing rhythms of life,
and like a shell residing in another shell of the body.
When there's no meaning whether it's night or day,
the season winter or spring, the vast ice caps melting,

ill-omened signs blazoned on earth and sky,
the tides in the city and the forests burning.

But hope comes in the faintest glint in the eyes
that one in such state will someday move to the windows,
open the curtains and gaze in rapture at the sun-drenched mountain.

The Mirror

Wipe every dust, every cloud from its face,
and the mirror reveals every line, every feature of vigor or decline,
and a hint of how we look deep inside.

The mirror shines no brighter with our beaming smiles.
No darkness crawls on it with our wretched looks.
It does not crack; it stays in its place when we curse our fate.

And when there's a deep gash on the face—
don't blame the fair mirror,
but the unsteady hand that holds the blade.

It shows the colors and adornments before we step on the stage,
but dares not hide the lines of unevenness, the furrows of age
before seventy seasons of summer have warmed our days.

Flickering Candles

We blow out the flickering candles.
We sing the wearied tune;
we ask where the years have gone.

But if we were to live the years again
there would still be cause to complain;
to bewail our fate and curse every bending lane.
"If only this could have happened"—
the most useless, despairing words spoken or written.

This precious little time—all we have.
What good it brings to waste the hours
with thoughts of what might have been.
Make the hours count; give them wings to fly
with a smile, a helping hand, a heart seeking to understand.

The wind beckons fair, the passage stands clear
when in the shadow of death—
we cling to no remorse, no regret.

People of the World

Look at the faces of people of the world:
menders of shoes, drifters who reek of booze,
people who never sow but reap
and those with wounds fresh and deep.

Folks who shout they were once swift,
but now lumbered on sticks.
Those with tattoos of dragons spitting fire,
interlocking vines and templates of erotic desires.

People who lay bricks, marble, stones and granite.
People who lower their nets in the silent waters of the night.
Those with dexterous fingers who scroll, search and type,
and those who would run many a mile to save a child.

See the children who play in the shadows of mud huts—
hands and feet tell stories of bruises and cuts.
And don't forget those who rest their heads on cold concrete,
and look at the stars and wonder if they too in the open sleep.

Ten Thousand Eyes

The masks we wear.
The smiles to hide the fears, a sea of tears.
The world little knows who we are;
we turn up in masks and costumes stretched miles afar.

The enigma of playing with masks—
those who know us the most hardly know us at all.
They see faces unsusceptible to an anguish or a fall.
And when the pain deep inside cries for relief,
we smile even more—we add layers to our masks—
to cover fault lines in heart and mind,
and say to the world it has never been so jolly and fine.

But what can we hide from Time's ten thousand eyes?
They see us through and through in the fading light.
Hold up to the world the mirror that's in your heart.
Time will mend every crack, remove every stain,
every scratch, every unsightly mark.

The Squirrel

I wished it had eaten the sun-ripened tomatoes and left no trail.
But it's easy to know what brought me such sweet travail.
It's the garden squirrel that tore deep into their flesh,
and scattered the wounded tomatoes on the deck.

The squirrel mounts the trunk of a cherry tree.
It reaches the top and grins; it sees the harvest it wrecked.
It mocks my angry shouts and fists; it throws a limb on my face.
And when I shake the tree, it sends down a volley of threats,
and from a little furry thing a belligerence I never expect.

But when it's on the ground and sees me around
it jumps over vines, iron spikes, rough walls and fences,
and wouldn't mind a tumble and a grazed tail
to be a mile away with plans for an assault on another tomato tree.

The Private World

Your private world
is all your own; your making and unmaking.
And unless you turn on the lights
it's a dark, dreary place there:
no ship plies along its lonesome shores
or look to those forbidden cliffs to rendezvous.

And expect none to fend or fetch for you;
there're no dwellers there, except yourself.
No mother, father, brother, sister, friend or teacher
dares to know or enter that world,
Every minute of every hour you bask in its glory
or manacled by chains of unmitigated pain.

When your private world bears little resemblance
to what the public knows of you then it's a burden
to bestride two opposing worlds with ease.
And when a current rages on the outside
and shows who you're deep down inside:
the world is shocked and people shake their heads in disbelief.

And you cannot run from your private world
thinking it's not there with the elixir of forgetfulness.
A thousand feet will follow you; a thousand faces will stare you,
and exult in your defeat until you come to know:
you're the architect of your fate.

Bubbles!

They're bubbles!
They're bubbles!
They're bubbles!

There's charm in these most ephemeral of things.
They rise and dance in the sun,
but the bigger they grow, the sooner they burst
into nothingness before our eyes.

Children have fun trying to hold them.
They want us to know they're mere fickleness
borne on the screen of time.
Yet, see how we labor to grasp the bubbles:
another name for the world's glitter and acclaim.

Labor hard and long but not for the bubbles of the world.
There's much to be said for the one who plods along
despite the derision, the ten thousand rejections
that cannot reach the fire in the heart that impels the onward call.

Think of those who labor in steadfast love
doing what they feel worthy as a calling from above.
They will not cease to labor because their names
not blazoned on the bubbles of the hour.

On the Wings of the Wind

The wind carries on its wings
the fragrance of daisies, hyacinths and jasmines.
With the same gusto and flair, its course set to the task,
it does not hold its breath or wears a mask
as it rides with the putrid smell of a bloated donkey
dashed on the rocks by the unruly waves of the sea.

The wind does not feel defiled when it crosses a loathsome path,
and thinks it strange that we run from it with abhorrence
when it's no different from the one that caresses the gardens.
And what the poor wind to do when we run
from the skunk, trash piling on the sidewalk,
a running, festering sore, every excrement, every infested pile of manure.

The wind was not born to fetch only what we embrace.
From whatever place a bundle it takes,
and sometimes on its shoulders rests the stench of decay.
The wind would its nature betray
if at the scenes of putrescence it were to veer away.
It may as well cease to venture where we dwell,
and cast a shroud of unbroken stillness over every gate, every well,
and then wherever we look—like the painting on the wall—
unmoving clouds and quiescent trees.

Walking Alone

I walk with bare feet on grass soft and lush
away and away from miles and miles of concrete.
My heart swells with the touch of soft dark mud.
In these lonely steps I find much repose.

The wild wind ruffles and spoils my hair;
unruly waves drench body and soul.
I am wary of forlorn faces and winding stairs.
See how the dark rain clouds are ready to pour.

From sweet pure rain I neither run nor hide.
Awakens songs of love in lonesome hearts,
and when the sun comes out and mocks the clouds
I toss aside all worldly doubts.

Sometimes we need to walk alone.
These steps are anointed.
They are lighthouses on the long way home.

The Measure of a Delight

Think of the poor and the famished,
and the circumference of the world they inhabit.
They have scant praise for the setting sun
if their feeble eyes dared to watch the celestial fun.
And what's the rapture in a rainbow
to those who have but ribs and sunken eyes to show.

They wait and watch with listless eyes
in a world of infestation and flies.
What's the hope in what life can give
when they cease to think whether it's better to die or to live.
And what's the good if flowers bloom before their eyes—
their children too weak even to cry.

When the blithe breeze plays on their hair
it lifts the dust that mingles with their tears.
The measure of their delight:
some lentil soup and boiled rice.
Those who feel unrelenting hunger and dampness in the ground
little know of the beauty of things around.

But there's hope that those who now cry for bread
would someday move to the beat of festive drums,
feel the touch of soft dew-laden green grass
and crave for the beauty that ennobles the human heart.

A Parting Gift

I gazed at the sun gradually sinking
into the bosom of the deep sea.
A fading lamp
but a thousand delights time compressed,
and in a span of moments:
a celestial blaze of the firmament.

A parting gift;
a bed of crimson red
the sun makes to rest.
The embrace and dance of color and light
like the distant glow of a forest alight,
Autumn leaves strewn in the sky
and infinite hues subdued and bright
streaming through scattered fabrics of clouds.

Compelled to gaze long
until that lamp was gone.
Still ten thousand shades of vanishing light.
Deep meditative silence fell on the land.
Then—
the majestic curtain abruptly closed:
darkness swallowed every trace of its eternal foe.

Insane Readiness

There's much shedding of blood in nature
in the hounding trails of tigers, lions, buffaloes and hyenas.
But it's from teeth, claws, horns and hooves into flesh
and not form bombs, missiles, and bullets.
Of all the things humans have stockpiled
no greater evil than these hardware of death.

There's something to be said of the state of the world
when peace rests not on words of accord from the heart,
but on flying demons bristling on launching pads of insane readiness.

Would that they were not in our fair world.
That the purveyors of meteors of death shunned
and reckoned deranged and demented.

And humans raving mad to kill in numbers
let them kill but with teeth, bare fists and feet
and not from a bunker ten thousand miles afar.
That the world be spared these rivers of blood,
fire, carnage, children buried in a rubble
and mothers wailing and beating their chests.

The Fallen Oak Tree

Its roots uprooted; it's a foul deed.
But there're no cries, no crowd gathers
and no voices raised at this insensate act of rage.

The wind saw blood on its hands and ran.
But who will apprehend a thing that rides unseen,
and miles afar fetches the fragrance of hyacinth and jasmine.

There's no obituary for the fallen oak tree.
No solemn march; no black ribbons worn.
There're no candles; no scribbled messages at its roots.
Not even a mark to show where it stood.

No one bids farewell to the fallen oak tree.
A thing that stood in beauty; a thing blotted from memory.

But the wrens, robins, sparrows and finches
stand in vexed silence; they gaze at the fallen oak tree.

They will find another but will long remember
that tree where they sang and darted from limb to limb,
and as fledglings saw the deep blue and broke the raging wind.

They seem to feel the pain that when a tree is felled
a thing of beauty gone and the world never the same.

Untouched by Time

On the shore in a far country
my heart floods with distant memories.
Refreshing breeze of the Atlantic wafted over my village.
Woods and branches drifted in aimless bundles.
The castles I built that waves dismantled in glee.

When the sun rose
I gazed at the gifted gold on the ocean's face.
Waves caressed the sand as in a musical interlude,
and when in convulsion they battered the shore:
mighty surges thundered and drenched my soul.

The beaten wall ceded in places;
timbers worn by barnacles and slime.
Roofs of zinc corroded by the salty mist.
Houses with tales of climbing vines;
sagging fences in haunted decline.
But that watery realm below the vaulted blue:
untouched by time.

Its pounding surf still enters my dreams.
Its mystical silence invades my being.
And when I sit in a meditative mood
the ocean rides with waves that soothe.

Unlearning

We learn much in schools.
Encyclopedias crammed in our heads;
a cluttering not seen in well-kept gardens.
Theories that make our shoulders bend;
conflicting arguments that stretch our wits to the end.

But much too to unlearn in that greater school of LIFE
whose walls extend far and wide
though not as imposing as unfeeling towers of learning.

That greater school of LIFE where few dared to enter,
and the best of students and teachers also fail
and the tailor and bricklayer outshine the lauded scholar.

Those who enter the walls of hallowed schools
just as likely to tread warily and stumble and fall
as those who learn in mines, factories and fields,
and in the drab dwelling places of the world
where joy mingles with the anguish of tears.

Why, then—
the mind-numbing listening, memorizing, recalling,
conforming in the suffocating air of grim classrooms,
and sleepless nights staring at glum, insufferable pages
when our education begins:
when we cease to walk along the corridors of learning?

Just for a Day

Just for a day
hearken to the call of sun and mild wind,
hum a song along the dusty trail,
make into one ball your worldly cares
and fling it far into the river's swell.
At the end of day when all is said:
no load on shoulders for you to pause for breath.

Just for a day
let your heart fetch the aroma of wildflowers,
the blissful face of the placid lake.
They displace the ill will for any human or beast.
And when you behold the cloud-drenched peaks
the wind aids your thoughts to lift above narrow
walls of pettiness, outmoded rituals and beliefs.

Just for a day
play and laugh like little children.
Open your soul for a drenching along the shore.
Fill your pockets with fat colored chalk sticks,
and draw pictures on the sidewalk:
people talking, blending, dancing, holding hands.
Relinquish that sordid style that speaks of a chain of command.

Just for a day
a little space from the wearied ways of the world

to befriend your soul.
A little more to see but with the inward eye—
to know the flowers before they die.
And the gathered sweetness of this one day
will impart its likeness to more of your days.

Holding a Pebble or Two

Who can tell the farmers, fishermen and bricklayers
life is nothing but one big, big unending dream—
no reason to aspire, plant an ambition, lift a finger—
when life stares them every day in every patch of field,
every turning of the tide, every block of clay
and when their lives rest on what they hold and fetch?

Who will furrow the fields,
lay the nets in the silent waters of the night
and set the stones on the resplendent dome
if they sleep the hours away thinking it's all a dream—
a folly to labor and play?

If you ever seek to know the mystery
whether life's real or a dream—
if you ever seek to fathom the depth of the open sea,
and measure the height when we look upwards—
it's better to begin reaching for the ceiling,
holding a pebble or two and smiling
while strolling along the splendid sea.

Telling Stories

Layered rocks, buried bones, bed of the sea—all venerable storytellers
They tell stories impressed on them a billion years ago:
strange faces, bizarre changes and vanished creature.
They don't distort or embellish with flourishes of their own
what the unerring hands of Time want us to know.
And if called to give testimony of our baffling world
would give a true account as only the voice of the Universe could do.

And we too like to tell stories,
but we make them taller and bigger like the shadows we throw.
We give to them much flair and color,
and add a hundred or more layers,
and in every telling and re-telling a new story born
like in the churning of the ocean new waves arise
to batter the shore and drench our soul.

The Blazing Chariot

The nights yield some ground
for the tall days around
with ice cream, sand and sun-drenched fun.
It's an early hour; folks still dreaming.
But the effulgent chariot climbing, climbing,
peeping through the dark curtains,
beckoning to behold the mountain drenched in molten gold
like the streets of El Dorado of old.

Tides come and go; friends bid goodbye.
The chariot still mounting the sky.
Wine-filled grapes welcome the exhausted day;
it's just the start of fair May.
Buttercups and lilies don their best dresses.
Vines emboldened to longer stretches,
and when the boy gathers the cows for the day:
the chariot blazing away.

A Stillness

Not a stir from leaf or limb.
The trees beg for a wind.
The meanest whisper of it will do.
They do not like to be mere paintings
staring at unmoving clouds;
looking down at the earth that seems to hold its breath.

A perfect picture
of a stillness no painter or poet can show on canvas or page.

But such stillness cannot last.
The wind has work to do.
The trees will not be transfixed in their places.

A flapping of wings, a wriggling, a stretching, a walking, a flowing—
at the very heart of things.
We abhor the stagnant drain; we rush to the gushing stream.

The Universe loves a rhythm and a dance.
All things must flex some muscle.
To standstill—too grave an ill to bear.

Don't Give up on the World

Don't give up on the world.
Every drop of blood, every tear shed
opens the flood gates of compassion
that surges deep in the human breast,
else every stream, river and sea will cease to flow,
and every day the sun a battered and bloodied face to show.

Hands lifted in noble deeds will long outlive
those wielding flashing blades and sending death
on the wings of bullets and blazing meteors in the sky.
Crawling vermin cannot bear a little light,
but the radiance in the human heart
outmatches the brilliance of a thousand stars.

A fiendish dance can never outlast
the march of human nobility well-bred and clad.
What's a brutish prattling to a great symphony;
a clogged drain to the expansive sea?
And what's a heart that delights to offend
to one that brims with love's magnificence?

Winged Beings

If we're winged beings born to fly
then why these sermons that decry
our fate and say we're condemned and doomed
even as we walk in the sun at high noon?

To be reminded of a treasure to reclaim
not the same as saying we're eternally stained.
And as we grope for the light within—
don't trouble our search with the vituperation of your outpourings.

Many would have our wings pinned to the cracked earth,
as if it's our natural quarter and berth.
Many would say all we can do is to bear our travails,
and soothe the wounds of a fate that's sealed.

But nothing written the mind cannot erase;
no unrelenting fate that cannot be breached and laid to waste.
And no cage or cell, no fetters of steel can contain the human spirit
that wills to soar to realms beyond the deep blue sky.

Butterfly on Shoulder

When I was a boy, fleet-footed and strong,
I ran after a butterfly that flitted with wings of scarlet sunset
and iridescent marks of green and violet.

When I fancied it within my grasp
it gathered speed; it lifted fast,
and not once my fingers glittered
with the golden dust on delicate fabrics
steadied by the music of celestial strings.

But now I sit and wait—
a heart less in beat and haste—
gazing at the clouds and the lake.
And as if by its own sweet device
the butterfly on my shoulder alights.

Clogged Drain

The clogged drain detained
in narrow corridors of unrelenting pain.
It struggles to bend its way
through layers of bloated frothy slime.

But dares to dream—
will mingle with a crowd in a dashing stream,
and somehow find its way
into the swell of a pristine bay.

On the Porch

Life is better on the porch.
No dark curtains to hide familiar faces,
hands raised to brighten the day
and send the cares away.

The wind brings the fragrance of daisies and hyacinths.
The sun blasts the fever, the ungainly pretense.
My eyes roam on the wings of a gliding falcon.
I listen to the silence—it's better than any human sermon.

I watch the clouds go.
They too mark the minutes and hours.
They too driven to some end—
they seem to know in their blissful content.

The mailperson comes with a smile.
Talks of grave and funny things for a while.
I feel that once familiar surge in my heart
when laughter of children rises from the school yard.

I watch squirrels mount the trees with glee.
Wish I were as nimble and free.
But glad to be on the porch,
and gather what my eyes can still search.

On Charts and Horoscopes

They say they can read my future like lines on a page,
and hand me the book of my life in colors matching and bright.

But on their celestial charts I see neither the expanding orbit
of my dreams where I see ever changing scenes,
nor that sweet little bird that sings in my heart before the day starts,
and that tells of lines, circles and numbers drawn on the sands
which the waves are wont to erase with delight.

That Wild Joy

The body no longer the friend I knew.
Oh! what vigilance to guard against what it may do.
Why these aches and pains when you were so true?
Why the hands of time turned you into a cunning foe?

You press your malice and weight against the mind;
you can little impede the sweep of the fertile imagination.
You mock every adventure, every yearning for that unexplored sea,
every step we take along the rugged barren cliffs.

But you cannot despoil that wild joy along the dusty trail
when I see a sparrow's nest on the fork of an oak tree.
It's the spirit of the child that rises, and longs for the call of the wild,
though my feeble eyes can little see the falcon gliding over the sea.

And when the battered body lumbers on:
the spirit of the child bravely sings along.

A Little Blue Speck

A little, lonely, hazy blue speck—
how the earth looks from the realms of the cosmic depths.

If one were to be placed at that awesome distant vantage point
vain and petty would seem our wars, quarrels and strife.

But on this little speck hate breeds, ambition rides,
and fires seldom cease to rage in towns and villages,
on plains and mountains and in human hearts
with those unsightly things within.

The oceans mere ponds; continents like rooms crammed.
A more than paltry perspective of where we stand.

And it's more than a little madness when we seek to hide the sun
not to see other humans around, and to revel in the darkness.

Gifts to Unwrap

Let your hours be ribbon-wrapped.
Colorful, neat gifts time sends
for you to unwrap.

With haste tear the tinseled paper.
Open each box with a child's glee,
and hold what's in for all the world to see.

And when your hours all have spent,
and you pass beyond the shadows of earthly realms:
time may have more colorful gifts to send.

A Strange Brightness

The light of the candle has gone
before the swallow declared the dawn.
But before it died it confounded the silence of the night.
The light rose with a strange brightness
not seen when its smiles animated the living room.

And it made me to think of the old man
who baffled those at his dying bed,
and the golden thread of his breath.
He was not dazed; his face was ablaze with a brightness
not seen when he hummed a tune along the streets and byways.

The defiance of the light and the old man
born of a glory to the end of time stands,
like the majestic beauty of the sunset before the sun is gone,
or that spectacular burst in the universe before a great star dies.

While the Falcon Soars

Sometimes we look back at how far we have travelled.
We still reckoned some days as dark.
But then—
the sun was just as bright,
sparrows sang into the night,
steel pans serenaded the crowd with festive beats
and leaves rustled in the blithe breeze.

But something in our minds hid the face of the sun,
and made mute the rustle of leaves,
drowned the sparrows' songs, festive steel pans.
In our wonted ways we put a damper on things.
We strangle the light and dwell in the dark.
We lower our eyes on the cracked ground
while the falcon soars over fearsome cliffs and rough seas.

This is your Day

This is your day.
Cram its hours with music and songs,
thoughts and words no less fruitful
than labor that furrowed the fields,
and hands lifted with bread
for those who intimately know the world's scorn and neglect.

This is your day.
Grab the hours to mend fences along the way,
befriend a fellow traveler, a wildflower,
share cherished memories and laughter.
Stamp on this day what's engraved in your heart.
Watch how the robins on the treetops dart.

This is your day.
Don't send it away like an intruder at your door.
This day has long waited for you.
Embrace it as your loyal friend too.
Don't lose it in self-pity, in regret.
Unfurl the sails for adventures ahead.

This is your day.
If you have nothing to do—it's fair use of the day too.
But be aware of the hour and the season.
The butterflies and the gulls know them well,
and if you happen to rest in a hammock by the shore

listen to the eternal music of the sea.

Such Sleep

The cat curls up on a bed of yellow leaves
along a beaten fence near a bending tree.
Its blanket is the blithe Autumn breeze;
its pillows are the rocks beneath the fallen leaves.

No one sings a lullaby to send it to sleep.
Yet, see how sound and still it sleeps
like dew that settles on the tip of a leaf
like the quiet of the sea in the deep.

If we could know even a paltry measure of such sleep
how less harrowed and weary our days would be.
We little rest on our silken beds, our pillows of warm velvet,
but endless twists and turns, as if bristled with thorns,
and miles and miles and miles the mind burns
before a little sleep touches down.

There's something unearthly in how the cat sleeps.
A star watches from the boundless deep.
In its track of matchless glory—
it too loves to snatch a stretch of such sleep.

Piling Up

We watch the snow piling up in fields, on sidewalks and steps.
It's nature's way of covering the cracks and unevenness.
And though we walk with watchful eyes and bated breath—
the ground is levelled as it gets.

We watch our years piling up.
But there's no magical sweep of a master's brush
to cover the wrinkles, the protruding vexed joints
or emblazon lines of vigor on hands
that they may wrestle the raging sea—
when now they labored with pain
to clear the waters of a bloated drain.

It's bitter-sweet piling up when the years have reached our necks.
A more than little forgetfulness of hurried days of unrest.
And though we walk with ungainly steps
we still long for the pearls in the ocean's depths.
We notice the clouds, the flowers on the windowsill,
a drop of water tottering at the leaf's edge.

With a bowl of fruits on the table, a guitar close to the heart,
what color and flair we give to life's tempo
still there for those who can straddle the floor.
We grab these days that keep running if only to know
what they are saying.

Little Things

Wave your hand and send a smile to the lady next door,
the old man along the street propping a sapling,
sweet child brightening the sidewalk with colored chalk.

There's a gathered strength in every smile and greeting,
and in the hearts of those around—
the feeling there's still a gentle side of the human being.

It's not a thing carried by the wind.
It endures beyond the day, the passing scenes
and the limits of the seasons.

A hug, a word of cheer or comfort, a laughter—
they sound the depths where anchors reach.
They matter far, far more than tinseled ornaments of the world.

And a little wildflower tucked into the beloved's hair—
if it were on a scale—
would weigh more than the gold of empires of old.

An Accord

Strange that people fight to reconcile;
exchange blows to shake hands.
And when they desire to make love
they start not with looking into the eyes
but with a quarrel and a fight.
And in the heat of battle they roll together with no less fire,
but with the amorous blows of hugs and kisses
and then the sweet moaning and panting for breath.

If only wars were so juxtaposed to peace.
That in the blazing trails of bombs and missiles
humans could roll together and pour their hearts for an accord.

The Giant Redwood Trees

The giant redwoods gaze over rivers and seas.
They hear bestial shouts, drums of battle,
clash of steel and blast of a thousand missiles,
but hold fast to roots amidst fiendish terror and cries.

They outdo faded columns of cities and towns.
Behold the stalwarts earth sends into the stratosphere.
Their foundations laid in the quiet of day and night;
colossuses wrought with no steel and bolted joints.

Their girth a hundred humans couldn't span;
their biceps twenty hills crammed.
With no probing cameras, they survey plains over the sea
and broken pillars of forgotten empires.

See their roots intertwined in a love divine.
An embrace that stretches a thousand miles,
and on such a love they reach for the cirrus clouds
with resolute outstretched hands.

Near, Yet Apart

The trees are noble; they grow with stout hearts.
Don't make deep dreadful incisions into their trunks.
They may slump lifeless on the lap of the earth
before they have given the measure of their worth.

You see no pools of blood; you hear no cries of pain,
no agonizing screams in the throes of death's blows.
But the mighty river sobs; the forest grieves,
and butterflies and birds lament the fallen trees.

The trees ask but for the songs of the warbler and the robin,
sunshine, rain and the mild wind.
Yet, lovers mend their ways with kisses under the trees,
and weary travelers find sweet rest under their inviting shade.

And if you count yourself as neither a lover nor a weary traveler,
there must be some love in your heart for the grace
and beauty of the trees when they stand near, yet apart,
and dance in the winds with no cue from humans or beasts.

The Call of the Trail

A respite from the oppressive air—
I venture deep into the winding trail.
The rugged lofty cliffs, the inviting breeze;
a gliding falcon mocking our cares.

Sweet the fatigue; behold the cloud-drenched peaks.
I listen to the silence that affirms the creed.
In the strain and fall I heed the onward call
lest my dreams be stalled by the cries of wearied feet.

Along the trail it's more than a little rest.
A repose on hallowed ground—the very air blessed.
Behold tiny butterflies, wildflowers along the lake;
listen to the unrivaled soundtrack of the robin and the thrush.

The tall oaks mark the trail with strength and grace—
greater the silence under their far-flung shade.
And here the mind leaps with delight, the heart rejoices:
the trail is a temple with a chorus of ethereal voices.

Faces

Never seen dahlias, daisies, daffodils, lilies and roses
with angry looks and vexed faces.
When they shrivel and die, we remember
how they smiled to every passerby,
every wearied traveler along the dusty pathways.

It's a burden to rage against the world,
kick every bending lane with a bleak face,
stare at the stars and curse our fate.

An ill-tempered face rebels against nature's ways.
When it's the accustomed look we show to the world
it tells of the mean estate of our being
that loathes to celebrate life's wellsprings.

It's a long trip with glum disconsolate faces,
but the sun runs with jolly spirited faces around
that bring the frolicsome wind and within the heart—
the joy of quivering strings.

More than Rest

It gives more than rest
along the city's gates or in a secluded cave.
It's a thing thrice blessed:
the sweet communion of silence.

It asks nothing from the world
but for its tumult and strife to step aside
that it may enter unaided by the hours
that burn our days and nights.

It's not there when we're alone
if we hear the clamor in the market places,
and make no haste to atone
for the rampant mind and the unrestrained tongue.

But it makes a haven in a spacious uncluttered garden
where we watch for every weed, every blight.
And it's not averse to walking with us along the city's streets
keeping our heads steady amidst the bustle and boisterous beats.

Mist-Laden Songs

I drink a cup of country lemonade.
I sleep far from the city's gates
in a hammock along the pounding surf.
I waited long for mist-laden songs.

I wake to the seagulls' call
away from noisy streets and shopping malls.
And when I stretch my limbs
and look for a window to open—
my hands touch the deep blue sea;
my face feels the frolicsome breeze.

Light Steps

They fetch a brightness wherever they go.
They loathe the tinseled praises of the world.
They crave no crowd, no cameras, no stream of admirers.
Would rather be with those who know the good Earth.

They carry no spikes; their steps are light
like morning dew on tender green grass.
They leave no rough mark, no trace of spite
when they bleed from the blows of insolent might.

They impress upon Earth all that's sweet and swell.
They know the call of the hour, the places to dwell,
the music, the songs, the rhythm and rhyme
and the best of summer's rich red wines.

There's no haste in their accustomed ways.
They never intended to chase the night or day.
Yet, can out-run the wild wind
to keep a pledge, to bind a wound.

They would rather be on ice and fire
than leave the stains of untrammeled desires.
They point a way; they throw a light.
They see the world through the eyes of a child.

Little Butterfly

A butterfly alights on a mango tree.
An unobtrusive visitor as could be.
What sweet burden a leaf to show
like the payload of a flake of snow
like dew on tip of a blade of grass.

My fingers hesitate to touch its wings
lest they besmirch delicate fabrics weaved.
What hands wrought such bedazzled artistry?
Our intricate needlework of glittering threads
ill compared to these silken wings of crimson gold.

The little butterfly in a dreamlike stillness.
A fragile thing but immovable at rest
as the leaf trembles in the wind's breath.
It tarries not long; knows 'twas born with wings and glamor
to cut the air in sunlight and passing showers.

Lifts from the leaf with breathtaking ease
like a gem studded with angelic wings.
A quick dash to a tree, hedge or climbing vine.
Another leaf or flower to feel its tinseled touch,
and adorned with the imprint of heavenly dust.

A Rare Picture

Before the break of dawn
many waited, waited and looked long—
not for the accustomed chariot
rising from the sea with a resplendent hue
but for a rare picture the Universe drew.

It rose on the horns of a bull
in a blaze of celestial fire.
It defied no natural law; it meant no harm
though a good chunk of its face was gone.

And in that instant, we abandoned thought.
We felt the mystery and the awesome power.
Gulls along the shore stretched their necks and looked.
Did they also feel the mystery and wonder—
something more than a rare picture?

The Atrophied Heart

Like the stench in a stagnant slimy trench
our loathsome feelings linger long
along the splendid thoroughfares
and narrow dusty trails.

The heart made to contain the ocean
dwindled to a paltry pond of vexed emotion,
and what mean warm current it holds
seldom reaches the lonesome shores.

The gushing spring that quenches thirst
never from an atrophied heart, a ground accursed.
Why this snake-like coldness, this numbness?
It's not life, but a painless death.

Who will shake us from this robot-like slumber
that we may feel and live the hour,
sing and dance in the rain?
We look to the new age bards to show the way again.

A Little Earthen Lamp

An earthen lamp burns bright and steady.
A radiant face with a thousand smiles.
To think that such a little blithe thing can obliterate
the primordial darkness thick and heavy in a forgotten cave.

A gentle wind embraces it with a kiss.
See how it dances in unearthly bliss.
But it cries for a place in your heart
when a cruel blustery wind passes.

Let it rise to reach the ceiling.
It burns the dross to which the mind clings.
Trim its wick; feed it well.
You never know what a little earthen lamp can tell.

They Work and Build Too

Behold the payload of a tiny ant.
Runs with a broad leaf, a sturdy limb
like a rivulet that snatches a mountain.

But the ants have no marching bands; they blare no trumpet.
There's no ground-breaking, ribbon-cutting ceremony
like when politicians with spades and blood on hands
raise clods of earth where a sprawling temple will stand.

The tiny creatures of nature work and build
in the manner of what snowflakes do
in the blast of wind, in the silence of night,
and before we know—
the ground covered with ten feet of snow.

What's in a Walk

A walk is more than beads of sweat on forehead,
steps we track, calories and miles we burn,
blood shooting through veins, joint and muscles that pain,
blisters on toes and battered boots we show.

A walk is a rousing and a rebounding when our spirits are down.
Greeting a new barber in town; seeing the flowers of Spring around
and trees we have seen ten thousand times—
to see again but with the inward eye.

A walk is watching gulls diving in the sea;
squirrels mounting tree trucks with glee.
Touching soft wet green grass and slippery rocks covered with moss.
Humming a song in the park; watching the stars when it grows dark.

A walk is keeping with the rhythms of rivers and seas,
the playful wind moving free,
looking at the changing clouds and the geese lumbering about.
A walk is beholding the magic in silent streams and restless rapids.

A Smooth Slab of Rock

Among its jagged friends,
a smooth slab of rock sleeps along the river's edge.
The unnumbered years the furious waves
have rolled over its sunburnt face,
and like the crafty hands of the potter
removed the indentations and the slimy spikes of strife—
roughness that tells of a hard forsaken life.

But now a pilgrim can stand on it at last:
a smile from a sunken face in the watery blast.

When the Pink Lillies Die

We don't hear the bells toll
when the pink lilies, the vines and creepers die.
While they live, they grow, bloom and run.
Now for a bigger pond, garden and field bound.

They don't leave with gloom and remorse,
a weary tale, a woeful discourse.
A longing for just another tomorrow;
another glance at the sky and the meadow.

Seems they are more eager than we to drop
the tattered coat for one that's new.
To leave a dried-up pond and cracked earth
for expansive waters and higher ground.

When there's not that brightness in their eyes,
and they feel the vexed joints, the labored breath
and know their days and nights are done—
they don't rage when called to the other side of the Great Divide.

The Dawn

Wake up!
No dream holds more charm.
Behold the dawn!
The lotus rises from the muddy pond.
What in all of nature to compare to this ethereal calm!

See Mother Earth in ten thousand robes.
Watch the playful battle of colors.
Tints of purple, pink, orange and crimson;
a mystical canvas borne across the sky.

The world stirs from its slumber;
cares little for this moving hour.
And in the slumber of wakefulness—
the celestial dawn vanishes.

But along the sacred river
a boatman bursts into songs of rapture.
A farmer trekking to his fields
lifts his hands in prayer.

A Stirring Speech

I listened to the deep and tranquil sea.
I heard no sound from human or beast;
there was no sermon, no admonition,
no raised hands on a lectern.
I saw no flowing robe;
I saw no beard white like the Himalayan snow.
No honeyed charlatan unraveled the mystery.

Yet, a stirring speech was uttered by the sea.
A message so clear; a message unerringly divine.
It needed no applause from human hands.
But there was a gliding falcon:
a stillness and a power in that breathtaking silence.

Unseen they Roam

Love the smell of newly dug earth
that mingles with the unspoiled air.
The smell of hot tar on road,
or to make sturdy the timbers of a boat.
The sweet blast of mint and basil
that floods porch with stories to tell.

Love the aroma of corn bread in the oven,
cheesy zucchini casserole, pumpkin pies,
tarts of pineapple, roasted nuts laced with honey
and drifting out of the windows—
inviting trail of sweet potatoes.

Love the fragrance of blooming jasmines,
violets, chrysanthemums, tender gardenias,
lotuses rising undefiled in the muddy wild,
and the scent of a summer's breeze
mixed with mud, twigs and leaves.

Unseen they roam,
but not with the freedom of the wind that gives them wings.
Yet—
they fashion my dreams; they awaken my desires.
They leave their imprint on my shoulders
after I passed the limits of their purview—
like the freshness of the spray that lingers in my breast
after I crossed the margin of the bay—
to contemplate the passing of the day.

Battle Cry

Exhort yourself to be battle-tested;
cringe from been battle-wearied.
Life's not a carnival.
No lesson garnered and no wind-swept mountain taken
when no wounds you carry,
and no severed limb tells of your bravery.

Don't tarry on the sands.
It's not the time to watch the clouds dance
when battle lines are drawn.

Keep sharp your wits; take the sun as your shield.
Draw the steel from its sheath.
Be ready for a charge with a battle cry over hills and sea.

Lost to Time and Season

The dust rises with a sudden wind.
On the rose tree the robin sings.

The little stream rushes to find its way.
The vine stretches in the night and day.

The gull spreads its wings over unruly waters.
The sea beckons mighty storms to gather.

They all keep watch over the bright North Star.
They hear the music of the spheres from afar.

They are acquainted with the hour and day of every season.
Strange we never reckoned them so blessed.

We trampled the dust, mock the gentle stream,
cut down the tree and blackened the face of the sea.

But if we dared to look into the mirror of our soul:
we would behold a being lost to time and season.

How the Trees Pray

No one teaches the trees how to pray,
but they do it well at night and in the day.
They pray when it's fair and when the storms rage;
they pray better than any wandering pilgrim or sage.

They don't step on any hallowed ground
or climb cliffs and traverse villages and towns.
A rush of wind is all it takes
for the trees to bow and beseech sweet grace.

And when it's calm and the stalwart trees stand tall in the sun—
they remain in prayer as when their limbs touched the ground

A Sweet Forgetfulness

The living things in nature—
they too bleed, suffer and grieve, tremble and fear.
And their greater fear not from raging tempests
or stealthy steps creeping in the tall grass,
but when they see the footprints of a human being.

They too mourn uprooted trees and vanished shores,
forests ablaze and the ocean's blackened face.
But they don't bemoan the ill winds of fate.
They don't dwell on wounds and scars of battles gone
or the greater battle when the morning dawns.

It's a blessing that shields them with a sweet forgetfulness.
And though they don't contemplate the Milky Way:
no leopard, falcon, or parrot ever trapped in the net of melancholy.

Along the Pavement

He staggered along the pavement clutching a small bottle of rum.
He faltered close to me; he had a story to tell.
He said with a smile but with a sadness in his voice:
"My friend, there's more than medicine in this bottle—
 it's the very elixir that saves me from the ills of life.

Early each morning I pay homage to it,
and when I go to bed at night it's this bottle, I hold still tight.
No teacher, friend or dear one has shown me the way
like the face of this bottle I behold each night and day."

Then I tapped him on the shoulder and said:
"Much of the world in some such state of drunkenness
though your much lauded bottle we may not embrace.
Our robot-like motions muffle the awareness of sun and season,
keeping us too busy and stealing our hallowed days.

How little we hear robins singing on treetops.
How little we watch daffodils dancing beside the lake.
And it would be a double drunkenness if we were to take
what's in this bottle to save us from the raging tempest.

Beware of a forgetfulness—sleeping at high noon—
lest, before we know, the sands are through the neck of the hour glass.
Break the bottle and with it the illusion of a carefreeness.
Life's a most precious thing to lose even for one priceless hour."

Moment to Moment

I keep a lookout from moment to moment.
I watch the spires of the churches,
the stalwart trees that would not reveal their ages,
the giant rocks at the river's edge.

I watch the hills, lakes, plains and mountains.
I watch the lighthouses and the currents of the sea
and those raging within me.
They all deceive with faces of permanence.

But from moment to moment:
it's not the same trees, lakes, mountains and sea,
lush plains and hills, the same vexing throb of the human heart,
the same twigs and leaves, fireflies that live but brief,
swallows on the tree, the same human yearning to be free.
It's not the same pages impressed with the wisdom of an age;
colors they said wouldn't fade.
It's not same thread on which hangs a pebble and a star:
the same love in the human heart.

A Defiance and a Flair

Every wind brings a different feeling;
every towering wave a different drenching.
Every mountain shows a different face;
every star a different brightness each night we gaze.
Every drop of rain hits the roof with a different beat;
every aging floor tells of its pain with a different creak.

Why then we move with the same strident steps
like machines that ask for little sleep and rest?
How we love to fall in line
like taking another road a dastardly crime.

Show a defiance with your own flair, style and color.
Rebuff every trait of the clan; every call that bends you to conform.
A thousand suns beckon not to cringe to an outmoded creed,
but to send your anchors deep and dream like only you could.

Voices

When the beauty of the pink lily,
the silence of the deep blue sea
and the obdurate strength of the mountain
enter like rivulets into our being—
we cease to dread the dire warnings
of voices echoing through the corridors of time.

We cease to hear the snake charmers,
conjurers of tricks, makers of magical potions and amulets,
and those who would dangle a sword before our eyes
and make us believe it were a garland of pearls.

And we cease to hear the ten thousand other voices
seeking to drown that little voice that's ever our own—
we heard loud and clear in our childhood
when we ran up the hill and kissed the clouds,
and never doubted what it meant to touch a blade of grass,
and anoint the feet with fresh earth before the day had passed.

Measure of a Day

Between the pillars of a sunrise and a sunset—
the mind takes hold; the mind dictates.
It's not the same state; it's not the same world
the mind begets.

The hours fly like a falcon over the sea.
The hours dared to stretch to eternity.
The heart leaps in music, dance and songs.
The heart sinks with the anchors of regret,
and the fears the imagination foisters on the day.

One falls into a deeper slumber;
the binding ropes drawn tighter.
But behold the untold treasures in a day
when the chains are broken and the sky opens
for a winged being to soar to worlds untrodden.

And so it's not the shadows thrown on the deck,
but the changing hues of the mind that tell of the measure of a day.

He Planted a Tree

The old man planted a tree in the park
in the shadow of a sprawling red oak.
When stormy winds shook it hard, he sheltered
it within the portals of his heart.
But the old man died before the tree grew tall.

He never took a little rest under its shade,
or looked at the nest the robin made.
Never saw its leaves turned yellow and crimson red.
Never saw squirrels mounted its trunk in blithe delight,
or the tiger moth butterfly alighted on its branch in blazing sunlight.

Never a witness to its impassive strength—
resolute in the fiery blast of the sun's wrath,
unrattled by storms and lightning strikes.
But the old man knew these things all along.
He would never see the tree sprightly and strong.

That's why he planted it with a song
that his spirit may live on in that which is suckled to the earth,
and for you and me and the world to see:
beauty of life that's in a tree.

Hands that Nurture

They speak the language of love in the form we know,
but then in a way baffling in depth and mystery—
it's still a secret in the Universe.

What in all of nature can speak softer,
and send messages with eyes and nurture with hands tender?

And who with one word, one look
can give to a lonesome heart such measure of bliss,
or send to crawl to the edge of the abyss?

We give them the first flowers of Spring.
We watch how they dance and sing.
They are more than the pupil in the eye;
we would wage a war against the world not to see them cry.

But, for some they are gilded merchandise
to trade in marketplaces in dollars and dinars.
Some violate their bodies and minds in bestial ways
that make the rocks on the hills leap in rage.
Some send them to dance before the lustful eyes of men
who interrupt the rhythm of drums and dancing bells
with the sound of bags of golden coins tossed on delicate feet.
And some send them to houses of ill repute.
The world then counts and measures the stains on their soul,
but not the poison they drink that the wretched hands of men pour.

The Swallow and the Seasons

The seasons seldom late or soon,
but the swallow at ease in the changing scenes
as when the leaves full of zest shine in their luxuriant green
or when every garden a blazing sunset
that lifts the faltering spirit of the fading days.

When the trees all bare and the air biting—
the swallow does not look back to the days
when the sun overstayed to gaze at the earth's face.

When snow covers roads and gates
and brings a stillness to the face of the lake—
the swallow shakes its feathers and makes swift
passage to a cozy barn on the farm.

There must be something that guards its mind
for it to perch so close to the edge of time.
And nature looks at it with unwavering eyes
because the swallow chooses to claim the day and night.

Bare Fists and Feet

Don't run for the gloves; show of what mettle you're made.
With bare fists wrestle with the crowds and noise
while you dwell in the stillness of the inward eye.

Don't hide your feet from the earth with layers of wool.
The hardened feet can walk on splintered woods and sharp rocks.
The acquaintance with iron spikes dulls the pain and annoyance.

Unless the fashioned clay is taken from the potter's wheel
and made to stay for a day in that searing house that's the kiln—
no ritual thread will adorn the clay pot's neck;
no sacred river will enter its mouth.

Put your hands on the blade; let the blood flows in rivulets.
Look at temptation straight in the face lest you see
a thousand damsels dancing in your secluded place.

Darkness comes when the sun runs away.

A Dream

In a dream I saw scented streets, gilded gates and walls
and fountains gushing with ambrosia.
But before my heart could rest in these unearthly delights
I saw vile fumes from boiling belching rivers,
a ghoulish dance of molten lava
and rains that came down in brimstone and fire.

But nowhere a robed winged being or one with crooked horns.
I pondered long where the devils and saints have gone.
Then a child of celestial charm whispered to me:
"People look at old, tattered maps to find a hell and a heaven.
But look deep within your very self,
and you will see the dwelling place of the devils and the saints."

Portrait of the Soul

The hands of an artist were moved by the Universe
to put on a canvas your soul for you to see.
A sketch of your very self that's hidden from seers and mirrors,
the scorching midday sun, glare of cameras and crystal-gazers.

Every hill and valley, every contour of your being,
every winged aspiration and every untrammeled desire
in fine sweeping lines only you could remember—
yet, baffled how lines of charcoal can breathe, bespeak and beget.

And when in day or night you looked at the frame—
you unmistakably saw yourself again.
A gleaming light from every merit gained;
a stain and blemish from every inflicted pain.
And you saw yourself not like a clay pot made and stamped,
but like a dune of sand sculptured by the raging wild winds—
a continuous making and re-making that's never really done.

Then—
would you in a frenzy destroy the portrait
because it showed how far you have strayed
or would you keep it as a thing that speaks
to you and shows you through and through—
not even the beat of your heart or your labored breath could do?

The Search

The journey is long and dreary
along boulder-ridden miles, lonesome woods and cliffs.
A thousand tumbles and a thousand pains,
but the river tarries not as it looks for the sea again.

The scent is lost on tangled turns
along rivers, wild woods and villages and towns.
The bloodhound stops and admonishes the wind,
but never forgets the work for which it was sent.

And when a precious way is lost
in the midst of a thirst and a windy blast,
and an unrivaled lotus in the center of our being
forgotten in the agony of the hour—
along the paths of ice and fire and through the iron gates of time:
we must not forget what we are here to find

Scattered Things

Do not delay the minutes and hours of the day
with sullen faces and methodical ways.
Why the haste for each thing in its place?

Let the wind scatter things on porch, windows and floor.
The child in you likes to play with scattered things.
Do not slight it with this smooth upholstered neatness.

The firmament smiles in every scattered star.
The earth smiles in every scattered leaf of Autumn;
every grain of sand blown from a mound.

Think of how many mountains were tumbled into the sea.
And when, like the sun, we scatter our warmth near and afar:
we can begin to dance with the stars.

Some Unfinished Work

I once knew these fields I roam,
these hills I kiss.
These lush pastures;
these restless streams.

I once knew the old churchyard
overgrown with vines and weeds.
The dam the sea has breached;
these coconut palms swaying in the breeze.

These faces seem familiar,
these muddy roads, bushes and flowers.
The very wind whispers to my soul:
"You have been here before."

But like an errant schoolboy
some unfinished work to complete.
Some lesson to learn
before my spirit moves on.

And where I go from here never written or told;
not privy to crystal gazers or seers.
I travel beyond their purview—afar

Medals, Insignias and Ribbons

The mockingbirds, canaries and cardinals sing day long,
but would not have their feathers hindered by bright ribbons.
They would be amused if they were pinned to their breast—
never dreamt of such things when they were fledglings in the nest.

The tiny ant runs with a branch.
With no blueprint, a beaver builds bridges and dams.
They never ask the world for a medallion,
an insignia, a ceremony, roll of drums, call to attention.

What's an acclamation to the mountain
that asks for a band of gold from the sun?
And though a mile of ribbons wrapped around a tree—
it bows to the mild wind, not our praises, our entreaties.

And to the sea an accolade is a laurel of lead
she sends to the darkness of her depths.
Yet, in mending a fence we raise much dust
for ribbons—ornaments on our chests.

The Train Arrives

The train arrives.
It's not a minute soon or late.
You strain for a last glance at a gliding falcon.

Don't delay.
Don't be so dazed that when the flags are raised
you have to be pushed into the train.

Don't look back at that battered field crowded with weeds.
You're headed for a place with a brighter sun,
and fresh fields to furrow in the morn.

Such Scenes

The gates are locked; the doors are closed.
The lens through we gaze are shut.
We raise no dust; we walk in no puddle or mud.
We ride over no Kilimanjaro.
We roam in no Serengeti to watch leopards prowl.

But we see a river of milk and a garden of celestial flowers;
step into another world through a window in the Bermuda Triangle.
We raise from the sea the pillars of Atlantis.
We see a fire through ten thousand mirrors.
We wrestle a buffalo and a tiger.
At the midnight hour we wake up the village.
See the men and women with bamboo sticks,
but all they hear are the snoring and the howling wind.

We chart no uncanny scenes in the mind.
Do they break the bars of space and time,
and rush uninvited to crawl on our pillows?
Do they arise from some regions within
that baffle our wits and take us on the edge of an abyss?

But they make us to wonder—
it's so easy to bring down a flock of flamingoes,
and walk through the gates of heaven.

Molten Love

It came down from the realms of celestial songs,
but lost its flair in the desert waste of human ways.
For eons it was meant to last,
but the molten love became an Artic blast.
One fateful arrow swallowed the fire,
and life's bliss drowned in the agony that haunts the hours.

They swore to guard till death the love
that keep in orbit stars and planets.
How little they knew fate would throw a chasm of ice—
two hearts to stand light years apart.
But memories bring flashes of days when the wind
could find no space in their tight embrace.

Flayed Tree

I feel for you, flayed bending tree
buffeted and brutalized by the raging sea.
Your busted joints cry out with pain.
No gull alights on your forlorn frame,
and when the waves send their sprays
they mock, not heal, the wounds of your beleaguered days.

You once stood as a tall oak
nourished by the youthful breast of the earth.
You hearkened to the primordial call of the sea.
In sun and rains you stretched your limbs and climbed and climbed.
But now the elements hasten your decline
as you wait and reckon the fading of your time.

Lines on the Forehead

The deep lines on the old man's forehead drawn by age.
For nine decades and more he gathered from the ocean's depths
though his pearls not as rare as those garnered by the sage.

But not one line furrowed by worries in the mind—
by looking back at sad ruins left by the cruel North winds
or by peeping over the tall sprawling walls of time.

Like the songbird that darts from limb to limb—
light and mellow the old man's heart.
Every bundle of worries he lets go to the wind.

Timbers and bags of bricks rested on the old warrior's shoulders,
but he would not trouble the mind to fetch a trembling twig of fear
lest it turns into a spiteful serpent or a sword dangling over his head.

A Lost Song

At its prime and at the very hub
just when it felt the stirrings of love—
the wind did not intercept that fateful flight
as it headed straight for the windowpane.

No more dash and turn and miles to burn;
its wings on the deck were pinned.
The heavy rains washed bones, skin, feathers, flesh and faded blood,
and my heart yearns for a lost song.

More than Words

They fall unto the page
like patterns weaved into a delicate fabric
like cherry blossoms scattered on the sacred ground.

They are more than words.
They are lighthouses along the vast sea
when they gush from wells deep within,

They are more than words
when they make us look into every throbbing heart,
every mighty river, every mountain from every vantage point
and to feel the golden thread that runs through all—
on which hangs the Milky Way and myriads of stars.

They are more than words.
More potent than healing balm or herbs.
They give to the weary heart the skylark's song, the lily's charm.
Send the sun's radiance to blast the citadels of nescience,
and rouse the human heart to untrodden worlds.

Things Seen and Unseen

The delights of the moment,
the season and things seen and unseen,
spring not from much learning, much searching
along the untrodden path to a secret doctrine,
a dogma or a creed, a point of view or belief—
but from the mind that has found its place
and rests at ease in a hammock near the pounding surf.

A greater conquest made without raising a voice, fist or blade
by the mind that surveyed where the world's eyes little gaze
but wherein lies the joys and sorrows of our nights and days.
The mind that looked into the eye of the storm,
and watched the walls of its self-imposed exile torn down.

And when at last in its own place—
it's unruffled like a lamp in the shelter of a cave.
And petty, vain and shallow all to which we cling
to the one who has found stillness within:
divine beyond the allure of earthly things.

Monuments of Love

When two lovers meet under the old oak tree
their warm embrace and kiss—
it's an unearthly bliss that stills the drums of wars and hatred,
broken dreams and sham in this world so vain, so sordid.

The world is weary of war but not of love.
Let there be monuments of love in every town.
Let the bell criers shout of love.
Let every pen be dipped in the ink of love.
Let every young heart dream of naught but love.
And if we would place a garland—let it be at the feet of love.

The roots are wrapped in love—
they send the giant redwoods a hundred miles above.
The river knows of love—
the struggles and pains it bears to merge in the bliss of the ocean's swell
And few would declare their love in songs that reach the hills
as sparrows and robins from dawn to when the night is still.

All of nature—a song of love.
Gentle waves caress the shore in a sweet love song.
The heartbeat of the Universe in every instance of love
that holds the atoms and keeps in orbit the stars
and anoints the human heart.

Not by Words

How little we say when we need recourse to words.
How much we say by holding a hand, cuddling a child,
tapping a shoulder, wiping a tear, sending a smile.

Not by words, but in the little things we do
that spring from the fount of silence—
make us to apprehend what moves the human heart and mind.

Not by words, but by planting a tree
we give to the world a thing of beauty
that will long outlive our wonted discourses.

Not by words, but by looking into the eyes
is love born and two hearts holding hands
facing the raging storm—an unfeeling world.

Not by words, but from the wellspring of a deep impulse within
the best of prayers we can ever say—
the most touching entreaty at the feet of the Universe.

And if we would live in fullness—
more than the insistent cue from words—
silence the assuring hand to take.
Silence walks beyond the threshold of the soul;
words keep knocking and waiting by the door.

What words can tell of the splendor of the sun-drenched mountain?
What words can tell of the music of the spheres?
The quintessence of things lost in utterance;
the rare bird gone as soon as we proclaim its glory.

No Story to Tell

There was a time when days were frolic and fun.
Every puddle a river; every rock a Gibraltar.
Every wildflower a precious thing to embroider the heart
and every clod of earth a universe.

Now we scorn the puddle; we trample the good earth.
When they bar the way, we blast the primordial rocks
and seal the fate of wildflowers and trees
with unending miles of asphalt and concrete.

Who feels the loss when we hear no babbling brooks,
no birds chirping in the woods,
when we see no dancing reeds along the river's edge,
no marching crabs when the tides leave the mudflats?

And the mighty river roars and swells,
but we have no story to tell.

Love's Pain

I hear the sounds of her ankle bells
though she's a thousand miles from where I dwell.
I am swept by a tidal wave of separation
and taken far, far from the city's gates.

I know not the hour, day, month or season
or feel the warmth of the midday sun.
I am dazed, but not afraid.
The caged bird has pity in its heart and sings a sweet love song.

The world little knows the lover's pain
and reckons these sighs are in vain.
But when the tide is gone and the wind is calm:
I will rest on my beloved's arms.

Over-Wired

We're ever so busy; we're ever so lonely.
A tiny screen has grabbed our minds,
and invaded the sanctity of our days and nights.
We're mesmerized; we're over-wired.
The mind charged with instant fires, instant desires.

There're photos we have air-brushed
as if we're sprinkled with celestial dust,
and time barred from touching our skin, sinews, and bones.
There's the convenience of "likes" to share;
all the things we want to hear.

Wonders how we once lived without this shiny screen.
But now the world knows our tastes, our fancies, places we have been.
We're data points, moving lines; we're followed, hounded like prey.
Where's that sacred space none dares to trace?

There's little time to think and feel the soft green grass.
To rest along the shore and listen to the pounding of the surf.

The time goes.
There's little family talk or meditative repast,
but furious fingers that scroll and search.
There's no warm hand to hold, but a slim screen that grows cold,
and a loneliness deep in the soul.

Listen

Listen to the silence
when the world is fast asleep and the stars awake,
Listen to that brief pause
when the waves break on the rocks,
the stormy wind shakes your heart,
and the church bells declare the hour.
Listen when the first snowflakes kiss the lake,
and the rain drops of Spring fall on the butterfly's wings.
You will hear what is beyond the spoken word.
The door of a temple will open.
You will enter into a greater silence,
but there will be no utterance from any priest.

Along the Shoreline

Don't walk along the warm shoreline in a flamboyant hat
or in smooth, elaborate garments.
The wind likes to play on your hair and skin.
There's little rhythm on felt, worsted wool and silk.

When it's bright and balmy—
why this gaudiness that suffocates the gladness?

The candor unfettered of layers of wool and princely gown
glides with ease over wind-swept cliffs,
and watches our fancy attire, dazzling diamonds and tiaras
as it kisses the clouds and soars over stormy seas.

New Year

The parrots, deer, dolphins, and kittens awakened and startled.
They wondered what's the cause for this cacophony
that rattles the quiet of the midnight hour:
clarinets, trumpets, horns, bugles, drums, explosive bursts of fireworks.
It's the New Year we ring in as we pop a cork from a bottle of wine,
and make resolutions that are drowned in the blast.

But the dwellers in nature don't bifurcate time.
They live within the circle of life; who can say where it begins and ends.

They reckon no months and years; they send no confetti to the wind.
They glance at no clock; they rush to the call of no hour.
And though time follows them in every track, flight and splash—
they hear no sound of a fast-approaching chariot.
They are troubled neither by remorse, nor forebodings of the morrow

Autumn

Autumn is the season to admonish.
Takes from the day when we love to play
as the sun in haste rides away.
A little sweat we break—creeping shadows come to say—
wings of night fast on their way.

Seems like yesterday they adorned the trees—
the rustle of leaves that brings cherished memories.
Full of life and zest, green and sheen;
proof against rains and raging winds.
But now their sinews drained and like fragile wings
fall at the slightest whisper of Autumn's wind.

With cunning zeal Autumn marches on.
Sparrows and canaries cease to sing along.
The frost that Autumn brings caresses
chrysanthemums with a deadly sting.
And a mighty shame to disrobe the trees;
send our feathered friends to cross stormy seas.

This Strange Altar

The fragile golden thread of our breath
can be cut at Time's slightest whim,
but how little we care from whence it came.

What is this strange altar on which we pay homage?
We reckon nothing is sacred; there're no anchors to steady the ship.

We splash all the colors on the wall,
and hope they would in immaculate patterns fall
to reveal the iridescent wings of the monarch butterfly.

We mock and distort every symmetry, every line of geometry.
We cease to hear the skylark's song, the rhythms of the sea.
Our loud drums frighten the squirrels and cause their ears to bleed.

We feel not the hunger pangs of those in far-off lands.
We disown the blood that drips from our brothers' hands.
And where's this interconnectedness—isolated we stand?

We build a house with no foundation; we build a bridge on no bedrock.
We give infallibility to this creaking stage where we laugh and cry.

The Band Plays On

Nature spreads a carpet of green.
Welcome to the wildflowers and the mild wind.
Trees smiling in their native regal sheen;
folks wending their way along dusty trails.

The long-slept seeds awakened with expressive life.
A profusion of splendor the perennial renewal brings,
and in the midst of our strife and bickering
tells of the eternal rebirth hidden in things.

That such dormancy springs to exuberance—
a miracle no less than if the blind are made to see,
and gives hope that in every falling and suffering
there's a season of Spring to blossom and sing.

The show begins with white, pink and red buds.
Eyes ready to open and tender leaves shooting out of limbs.
Then fragrant blossoms and the burst of flaming azaleas,
blooming hyacinths, violets, rhododendrons and tulips.

A band strikes up with mellifluous melodies.
Wrens, sparrows, robins and finches open their hearts in songs.
When it's the season of fertility and life's short
they will not just sit and wait on treetops.

The band plays on when the crowds have gone.

It plays for lovers and the weary in mind and heart.
It plays for those who stare at the night sky and hum a song
and inhale the fresh mint-laden air.

I long for the outdoors in the Spring to hear the laughter of children,
to see smiles on the faces of people—a little human warmth
to mingle with the aroma of chrysanthemums.

An Affirmation

To be cynical about love is to be a stranger to life
whose secrets more likely to be revealed in an embrace and a kiss
than in the mortification of the flesh—the denial of life's bliss.
Shorn of love, it's a world of vacant stares and the rivers hard to follow.
It's the balm that gives a spring to our steps—makes the heart mellow

Look for the star in the beloved's eyes
before you hunt it down from the unbounded sky.
It's a razor's edge you walk when your mind recoils
from what keeps the robins and sparrows singing into the dark.

When love beckons, walk as if in a temple.
It's the winged-chariot that leaves behind vexations of the spirit.
And to be in a warm bed in the beloved's arms—
not a forgetfulness of a world in the icy winds of unfeelingness,
but an affirmation of what the Universe declares in celestial songs.

My Love

What a thrill to hear the sound of your ankle bells.
I will not fetch you the moon— it's a barren place.
The rocks will offend your delicate feet;
the bleakness draw a frown on your face.

You will dwell in an enchanted garden in my heart,
and walk on petals whose freshness will remain
like the fragrance the musk deer carries along the mountain slopes.
And there in my heart you will know of a love
that's in every drop of the rain of spring,
every stream gushing from the mountain,
every daffodil dancing in the frolicsome wind,
every ray of the sun and every breathtaking scene.

New Eyes

A troubled young woman went to a far-off land.
She hoped the idyllic scenes would bring cheer to her mind,
and blunt the fears of her disfigured memories.

No burden of things to fetch;
she walked with such sweet dainty steps.
But she took with her the self-same mind
with the excess of its grip gathered through time.

The scenes of charm and beauty passed before her eyes,
but did not touch one chord within her heart.

If only she had known—
what we need sometimes is not a change of scenery,
but new eyes with which to see.

Entrenched Feet

On a swollen bed of compost
a tiny seed opened its heart to the sun.
When the rains came, its work was but half-done.

It defied wild winds,
thunder and flashes of lightning.
It became a little tender tree.

But its feet entrenched, it gathered strength
and climbed, and climbed and climbed.

It looked around and saw the mighty river—
thought the sight was worth the labor.

Awaken by Songs

No sound of human or machine—
no alarm rudely shattered my dream.
I awoke to the sounds of orange-breasted robins.
Sweet music rippled from the top of the tree
that guards my window with its sprawling reach.

What rousing songs from my feathered friends
to blunt the fears the day may send.
What respite to my ears, and to my mind—
sunshine to the mist of worldly cares.

I long to gaze at their frolic and fun,
but I must make worthy my tongue—
songs of praise for the effulgent sun.

Unfeeling

A numbness has taken hold of our minds.
In villages and towns we watch this wretched decline.
At high noon we walk like machines.

A young woman slashed a thousand times.
Trees lowered their heads and cried.
A crowd of humans stood by and watched,
but not one came to her aid
as she pleaded with every faltering step, every fading breath,
and crawled in a pool of blood to die at her own doorsteps.

But then I think of the people who risk their lives that others may live,
and a hope rises in my breast that this unfeeling spirit will fall off
like leeches dropping from the skin.
And when the steel goes into another's flesh
we will feel the sharp throbbing pain,
and see our own blood dripping on the stairs.

Cell of Rage

In a year the black hair of youth turned grey.
Somber lines on face drawn; he stumbled like an old man.
For forty years he never saw the rising sun.
For forty years he never broke bread with a human.

His companions were the dreaded silence,
unremitting darkness and howling winds.
He raged and raged against his fate.
There was no rage left in his heart to burn.

He sank unto his knees
and prayed, and prayed and prayed.
But each ray of light into his cell
turned into a darkness sinister and bleak.

He dreamt of the world taken from him:
the sunset, a gull gliding over the cliffs,
the embrace of a maiden and a sweet kiss.
But the cell mocked his every dream—
the bars of steel grew taller with each tortured season.

And when he was exonerated and walked a free man—
he gazed at a world he could little understand.
The forests were gone.
He saw miles of gleaming asphalt and concrete.
Ribs of steel stretched into the clouds.

Jets screamed over his head.
A screen he held—a tablet.

But forty seasons of sorrows drowned
when he saw the face of the resplendent rising sun.

Fire and Blood

When the nature of all things is to change,
why for the wretched of the Earth— it's just the same?

I rage and rage.
Can find no way but with outbursts in verses.
There's fire and blood in every line
like the outpourings of a revolutionary
to burn every rotten edifice, bury every stench
that makes the landscape a bleak hideous face

I know the stern faces, the contempt of the taskmasters,
the hard labor and the sufferings of my ancestors.
Every lash on their backs still cuts my heart through and through.
I see in my mind's eyes the white mansions of the overseers,
and (like a world apart) the barrack-like huts of diseases and discontent,
and a little forgetfulness in music and drums
my ancestors brought from their native land.

Though the absentee planters and overlords have long gone,
a flag unfurled and a new nation born—
I see strange boots trampling the ground,
mocking all we have won,
and in many a far-flung land, local governance gone horribly wrong.
The gall twice bitter to drink drained from plants grown by native hands.

I rage and rage.

Can find no way but with outbursts in verses.
There's fire and blood in every line
like the outpourings of a revolutionary
to burn every rotten edifice, bury every stench
that makes the landscape a bleak hideous face

When the nature of all things is to change,
why for the wretched of the Earth— it's just the same?

To Kiss the Deep Waters

Never heard of a vine wrapping around itself
and snapping the thread of its life
or a buffalo splitting its heart with its horns.
Never heard any bird, beast or insect
placing a noose on its own neck,
drinking a lethal cocktail it has made
or pointing a loaded gun at its face
or jumping from a bridge or cliff
to kiss the deep dark troubled waters of the lake.

There's something that guards the dwellers in nature
from brooding on the overflowing of their agony
that the thought never crosses the portals of their minds
to end it all with a gruesome show—a telling blow.

It's a shield not given to humans.
And thought we contemplate the Universe,
strive to reach the unreachable,
attain the unattainable,
know the unknowable,
yet—
we're prone to sweat on such sickled thoughts
that if unbridled for long can make us sink lower than anchors fall
as to loathe this most priceless of gifts and driven by a compulsion—
to smash the very gates of LIFE.

In a Saffron Robe

Today I wore a saffron robe.
With matted ropes of hair, beads wrapped around arms,
sandal wood paste in triple lines on forehead drawn
and holding the effulgent pot with the seven sacred rivers—
I walked along the dusty streets of the village.

And young and old with folded hands pleaded:
"Come Oh! holy one into our homes
for us to wash your feet,
that you may bless us with what we seek."

And then in a solemn tone I replied:
"I am now no different from the one
who walked your streets but yesterday
not in sacred garb but in a tattered coat.
Then you mocked and chased me away.
And it made me to wonder
what evil my disheveled face wrought
that you ran from my path."

The News!

I wish I could get the news of the day
from the fast-moving currents of the sea,
clouds that look down on plains and mountains
and the sun that sees into the heart of all things.

I rage against news removed from the scenes,
and then filtered through a thousand lenses
that tells of a raging storm
when we hear the beats of festive drums.

The people, places and seasons have changed.
There's a new song; there's a new beat in town.
But it's the same, same news I read and hear today
covered with dust and grime on faded pages stacked away,

If they had their ways, the eyes would fancy the placid lake,
the ears the song of the nightingale,
rather than the news with a litany of sordid details:
graft and greed and corruption and nakedness in high places.

Our hours trampled; our dinners desecrated.
The rich colors of the window curtains faded.
The enchanted light music in the background drowned
by bursts of gunfire and then the screams and the sirens.

The mind rebels; the heart sinks.

Show us even a glint of human goodness in the world.
Let not our dreams be fashioned on a fabric soaked in blood.
I wait and hope for news that tells it's such a beautiful world.

A Cap and a Gown

Look at the sullen faces of children and adolescents.
Have been told they must shine no less than the stars—
an encyclopedia crammed into their heads.
They must fly through the city's gates and walls,
and be walking templates of what it means to never fall.

But it's the slipping and falling that inspires the onward climb.
The river tumbles along cliffs in its search for the sea.
The waves rush again and again for the high-water mark.
Should the young in one fell swoop snatch the stars?

We fashion our dreams on the hours they burn;
we adore their medals and citations that adorn the wall.
How little we care if they would rather ride with the wind
with a new beat and tempo, a new love song to hum
or to see the swell of the river when the moon in exultancy
traverses the heavens unbesmirched by the presumptuous clouds.

Nature knows them far more than we do.
Nature knows them far more than we do.
The earth wants to feel the soft touch of their feet.
The wind calls them out to play; the rain calls them out to dance.

When we rob them of life itself—
what recompense there's in a cap and a gown?

A Strange Poem

An old man wrote a poem with words that gushed from his heart.
The poem became a living thing
that looked deep into the soul of every being—
the slightest ruffle of disquiet, the faintest gleam of light.

When it was read in the quiet of the day or night
the words and the lines were charged with a strange power.
The rhythm and rhyme changed at every turn of the hour.
The voice of the poem was never the same to each reader.

Each saw a different coat of blue on the firmament,
a different face of the mighty river
and looked at the mountain from a different vantage point.
The very world took on a different hue
and so too the past and present, and the old and the new,
and to each reader the poem was a mirror
that opened the heart through and through.

One felt the pathos of a haunting melody.
One raced on wings of the skylark.
One saw a dried-up pond; another gazed the glory of the dawn.

Phantom Forms

We carry deep wounds from sharp arrows
that never reached our shores or from any quiver sent.
Phantom forms of our beleaguered days and nights
shoot down the midday sun and make us to sleep
on broad stormy beds of jagged spikes of steel.

We give form and flesh to the unreal the mind begets.
We feel the sting though no cobra raises its head;
we hear howls of jackals in a field of sunflowers.
We invite into our scared dwelling an imaginary thing,
and give to it the power to make a bitter winter of spring.

A Little Knowing

When we work but not like the oxen
that pull the punt laden with sugar canes.
When we walk on the dusty plain
but not like the geese that lumber along.
When we look to the sun
but not like the vines that look too—then run.

When all the things we do
and all the thoughts we weave
stand on a higher point of view—
there's sure to be a little knowing
and what's more—
an awakening that a current runs deep within.
That we are linked as kit and kin
to every living thing in air, on sea and land,
to every gurgling stream, every valley and mountain,
every pebble, every bending reed, every cedar tree.

What's that Love

When eyes never did meet,
and words never did cross the frontiers of the heart?

A love that's more than love
when hearts and souls bonded
on a hallowed ground where silence resounds,
and time and space dissolve in an ocean of oneness.

I am drowned in that love.
I hear no ankle bells,
but a face comes up like the sun in the sea of my mind

The Old Man and the River

And I said to the old man:
"You have dug wells, given the harvest to the poor,
wiped the tears of fathers, mothers and children.
You carried a smile along the way
that illuminated the minds of young and old.
You planted trees and cared for the good Earth.
You are a lighthouse that guides us on the vast bleak sea of life.

Yet, I don't see your name on any cornerstone,
or engraved in gold along the city's thoroughfares.
I see no mention of your deeds in the wearied news,
and in your room, I see no trophy, no medal, no citation, no ribbon
blazoned on the wall that tell of the good you have done."

And then the old man replied:
"Son, behold how the river swells on this full moon night.
What would it gain from a pond that trickles in its mouth?
It fills the streams and trenches around,
but they know not of the reach of its silent depths.
The time-honored river is content to gaze at the face of the moon,
and when morning comes—it knows there's work yet to be done."

Can We?

Can we with nets flung far and high
catch a flock of flamingoes in flight,
or with outstretched palms gather the rains that drench the land
or the endless sands that mock weary caravans?

Can we with a golden arrow
gouge the eye of the approaching storm,
or with pens held high
write forks of lighting across the sky?

And can we with logic and eloquence
dared to enter the temple of eternal radiance?

Heat Wave

It's not the same sun of our childhood days
when it warmed our hearts, made strong sinews and bones,
healed bruises on knees and watched with glee our frolic and fun.
What have we done to provoke the sun?

Some days the fire in its eyes reaching the ground,
burning forests, melting roads and bridges, blasting towns.
Where's that shield, pristine through the ages,
to guard against this seething wave of torment
sapping the vitals of humans and beasts as we implore
the heavens to open the gates with a flood of relief?

People jumping into the ocean, rivers and lakes at high noon.
Who would not delight in a splash when the air a boiling cauldron?
Who would object when some bare it all;
when every undergarment feeds fire on skin?

What dreaded face the sun will show in a hundred years?
Will we ever learn; will we mend our ways?
There's hope that the effulgent orb from which life springs
will guide the hearts and minds of human beings,
and show again the face that warmed our childhood days.

Out of Tune

It's spring.
A renewal bursts in songs and color.
Behold the smiles; hear the voices of nature's choir.
The very air calls out to you.
The love birds beckon you to the outdoors where daffodils bloom,
and the air frolicsome along the bay at noon.

But you are out of tune with nature's charm.
You're not that jolly spirit the world knew all along.
Your face bears the imprint of some ailment within
even when the mild wind plays on your silken dress.
What has drained your hours of every song?
What has laid siege to the citadel in your heart?

Don't sit alone gazing at the bolted door.
The world doesn't like to talk of unseen wounds.
But you have trusted friends.
They would reach out to you with wings:
the sun, fields, hills, mountains and fresh air—
they have taken many over darker and more troubled waters.

When you Walked in their World

To those who govern
and from raised platforms look down at the people—
crawl into the skin, mind and heart
of those who suffer hunger, oppression and penury.
Stay there for a full year or two
to feel the only world the poor can ever know
that it may be as real as your hands that held the sacred book
upon which you swore to serve and keep the oath of office.

Take some of their blood and tears to be the ink to write your laws,
and when you seek to twist and bend a word or two
to serve might and power and disown the poor—
think of the time when you walked in their world.

A Rush and a Splash

We dip not gently into the sea but with a rush and a splash,
and not content with ripples to make
we send boulders down to trouble the face of the lake.

With much disquiet and haste we barge into nature's temple.
We trampled the sanctified ground, and with the noise of a carnival
drowned nature's celestial sounds.

Who protests the assaults on this last bastion of silence?
And when this too is gone—
the loss as precious as the nightingale's song.

Beginnings

The beginnings of things—
not a flare sweeping across the sky, a tempestuous roar, a swelling
but a trickling, a faint stirring, a low crying, a pleading, an urging
that little resembles what they are destined to be.
The unsightly chrysalis so different when it flies out of the cocoon
and alights on a lemon tree on the wings of the monarch butterfly.
The tiny stream, almost imperceptible and unseen,
dripping from the loins of the Himalayas—so different from the Ganges,
and the seed in the silence of earth so different from the giant Redwood.

The beginnings—slow and tentative—not furious and swift.
The jet needs to walk and run for a while before it blazes across the sky.
The white lilies bloom not in an instant but by degrees,
and so too the healing of a wound, the yearning to be free.
It's a gentle breaking and then the majestic black stallion galloping
as if from an unearthly breed it came—
its feet seldom seem to touch the dusty plains.
And what's a marathon but the steady building of a measured pace,
and when the bell rings—a burst of blazing glory to the finish line.

There's something to be said of that beginning
that's a little striving, a little seeking, a little longing
that though hidden from the eyes of the bustling world
often unlocks the secrets that baffle the fleet-footed and quick-witted.
And though all things must fade and disappear—there's something
that brings a faint beginning and impels the Universe into being,
as the widening circles of a ripple often begin
with the throw of a smooth pebble.

To Write and Erase

I am a child who has just begun to learn,
to write and erase.
Someone guides my unsteady fingers
as I trace the orbit of a star.

I have yet to learn the ways of the world, the ways of humans,
the vexations of their spirits, the fires in their hearts.
But I know the rolling hills, the fields, the dew-laden grass,
the gushing streams, the faces of the river, every wildflower
and every bird that breaks the stillness with a song.
They all give a contentment that feeds the hours.

Is this the closest I may ever come to feeling that uninhibited bliss
that eludes the heart and mind as soon as we begin to speak of it?

There will always be a child who has just begun to learn,
to write and erase.

Songs of Hope

In the unrelenting darkness in the earth
the tiny seed sings a song of hope—
it will be a giant oak.

When gentle reeds at the river's edge
bend and fall to the raging winds,
they sing songs of hope—
they will rise again, a little dazed,
to gaze at the sun's face.

And when the world on the edge of an abyss,
and we tremble to look at the clock lest it shows a bloody face
and with faltering steps we behold the wreckage before our eyes
that springs from the hardness of human hearts,
then like the tiny seed and the reeds at the river's edge—
we need hope when the fears seem too heavy a bundle to fetch.

Unbridled Waves

The shore seldom remains unscathed
when the unbridled waves
(born in the distant commotion—the churning of the ocean),
gallop like mighty thoroughbred horses to batter the defensive wall
with the fury of ten thousand hammers that fall.
And I feel for the hapless wall and shore;
the telling lashes and blows and the gore.

The violence drowns the stillness of the night
as the blithe-faced moon emboldens the waves to greater heights.
And I dream of sunken ships,
and treasures guarded by the silence of the ocean's depths.
I dream of sailors buried in watery graves,
and the brave who for the thirst of sea still crave.
I dream of the ocean incensed by the indifference of humans,
and coming to reclaim the land
and the people running, raising their hands.

A Line Above the Waters

A bird skimmed over the river—
steady like a fleet-footed impala.
It drew a line above the waters
like a blazing unerring arrow.

I held my breath.
The thrill in my breast—
magic, power and symmetry in wings outstretched.
Yet!
the inexpressible wonder of motion in rest.

It gathered speed over deeper restless waters.
Kept pace with it for miles
until it became an ethereal thing
moving in my mind's eye to a resplendent shore.

Seen many of its kind
but none so exquisite and sublime.
And it raced to my mind that when I ride waters dark and choppy
to think of that bird of peerless grace and majesty.

But now I must wait with eyes keen.
If fortune favors with a visit again
may it kiss the waters in a majestic swoop.
I wish to pay homage to that blithe spirit
that touched a chord deep in my heart.

A Ship out There

There's a ship out there.
She rides the sea with such ease.
The waves climb to break her bones.
She shows a steady bow and stern.
Bestrides the danger with composure.
An unyielding power in her keel
to reveal nerves of steel.

A rare courage and defiance
to a sea angry, restless and malevolent.
No blast from wind or wave,
no surging current in the dark depths
to dampen her spirit and delay her course set.

On the sea of life straddled before our eyes
like that ship we must ride.
There're bound to be storms,
billows, whirlpools, currents swift and strong
and a thousand things may go wrong,
but we must sail on,
but we must sail on.

About the Author

Haimnauth Ramkirath was born in the Republic of Guyana, perched at the very tip of South America. He grew up in a small village of rustic beauty and charm, where the rhythms of life were simple and predictable. As a child, he immerse himself completely in the fascination and beauty of the natural world. This love for nature is still one of the abiding joys of his life, and is reflected in many of his poems.

Haimnauth was a teacher for almost ten years at the secondary school level in Guyana. He came to the USA in 1991. He is a professional Accountant who has worked his way up to the Controller level. He lives in Bayonne, NJ with his wife, Radhika, his daughter, Tamala, and son, Akash. Haimnauth is an ardent practitioner of Meditation and Yoga.

Haimnauth has published four works of poetry: *At Ease Like the Blooming Lotus, Troubled World, Rhythms of Ease & Wonder*, and *Unsung Verses*. This is his fifth work.

www.ingramcontent.com/pod-product-compliance
Lightning Source LLC
Chambersburg PA
CBHW030038100526
44590CB00011B/250